the Magical Language of Others

a memoir

E. J. KOH

TIN HOUSE / Portland, Oregon

Published by Tin House, Portland, Oregon

Distributed by W. W. Norton & Company

Library of Congress Cataloging-in-Publication Data

Names: Koh, EJ, 1988- author.
Title: The magical language of others : a memoir / E.J. Koh.
Description: Portland, Oregon : Tin House, [2020] | English and Korean.
Identifiers: LCCN 2019031239 | ISBN 9781947793385 (hardcover) | ISBN 9781947793477 (ebook)
Subjects: LCSH: Koh, EJ, 1988- | Koh, EJ, 1988—Correspondence. | Koh, EJ, 1988—Family. | Mothers and daughters—Biography.
Classification: LCC PS3611.O3659 Z46 2020 | DDC 813/.6—dc23
LC record available at https://lccn.loc.gov/2019031239

First US Paperback Edition 2021
ISBN 9781951142278 (paperback)
Printed in the USA
Interior design by Jakob Vala

www.tinhouse.com

"A lyrical and profound personal excavation."
—BuzzFeed, Most Anticipated Book of the Year

"Exquisite."
—Lit Hub, Most Anticipated Book of the Year

"A powerful look at family, culture, language, and selfhood."
—Book Riot

"A cinematic and multigenerational saga."
—*The Stranger*

"Magnificent. . . . This is a memoir that
needs to be read more than once."
—*International Examiner*

"A haunting, gorgeous narrative that
is lonely but lushly told. . . . Brilliant."
—*Star Tribune*

"A beautiful, scorching memoir."
—*Chicago Review of Books*

"A masterpiece, a love letter to
mothers and daughters everywhere."
—Shelf Awareness

"A coming-of-age story, a family story, and a meditation on
language and translation, with an emotional range to match."
—Caitlin Horrocks

"Give yourself over to her narrative territory and the resetting
of the borders of lineage, language, and lives lost."
—Shawn Wong

A NOTE ON TRANSLATION

My mother opens her letters in Korean, *Ahnyoung*. This translates into *Hi* or *Hello*. I use both for the Korean greeting. *Hi* beams outward like the sun's rays. The tone transports energy without expecting reciprocity. One may absorb *Hi* with a casual wave or respond with a smile. *Hello* boomerangs for a response. Over the phone, one says *Hello* to hear a voice calling through silence. *Hello* is an alteration of *Hallo* or *Hollo* from Old High German *Halâ* or *Holâ*, used to hail a ferryman. *Hello* comes as a question. *Are you there?* *Hello* fetches me across an expanse of water.

Eun Ji is the name she gave me. Eun, as in *mercy* and *kindness*, closer to mercy than kindness. Eun falls between *blessing* and *blessed*. Ji lands at *wisdom* and *knowing*. Ji resides with *judiciousness* more than *intelligence*. Eun Ji does not echo willfulness or innocence. It resonates with softness and sensibility. Angela is my Catholic name, after Saint Angela Merici, a holy messenger. My mother calls me Angela when she speaks formally. Angela is proper for its foreignness—postured for the public. Eun Ji belongs to her. Angela, to everyone else. She calls my brother Chang Hyun, his Catholic name John, or your brother. For my father, your dad. For her, she is always Mommy.

Mommy addresses a child, who remains one in her letters. This becomes clear when she switches to third person. *When you feel a little better, if you want to talk to Mommy again, call me.* Her third person is, in part, her mothering.

Since my Korean was limited when I was a child, she uses kiddie diction. She stays mostly at a basic level. For advanced vocabulary, she transcribes the first definition in her English dictionary and notes it in parentheses in place of or next to the original vocabulary. *Auntie must get jealous* (envy) *because I have my Eun Ji.* Translating is problematic for her, but also a treat. The letters note, at times, the wrong English definition. In one, she means *promise* and next to *promise,* she writes *confirm* but misspells it as *conform.* She says, *Promise* (conform) *and say it to yourself.* Her error becomes a delight that cuts tension, or stalls grief. In another, she defines *promotion* as *propaganda.* She writes, *I have to assert and promote myself* (propaganda). Her language slips out of a perfect transcription and gives relief with its obfuscation and humor.

Words she writes in English or changes into Korean English are italicized in the book, such as *last of my life* and

God is *fair*, you know. Japanese words she writes in Korean are romanized: *Nani ga hoshii desu ka?*

Korean phrases are a favorite. *Aja, aja, fighting!* Not a signpost that signals transition between parts, this translates into *Let's go, let's go, fight!* The phrase uses the English *fight* or *fighting*. *Aja, aja* is a sound of activity, quick-footed, rising from the gut. Together, they bolster fortitude.

Readers may ask whether I wrote her back. Her letters are a one-way correspondence. The thought of writing her was unbearable. Korean was a language far from me. I never suspected I would come to it in the end.

The letters are included in their original form and not all appear in chronological order. Some letters have dates for meetings that happened at different times.

To my limits, I do not see my translations as complete. If her letters could go to sleep, my translations would be their dreams. The letters transport my mother to wherever I reside, so they may, in her place, become a constant dispensation of love.

Forty-nine letters were discovered after an unknowable number had been trashed or forgotten. In Buddhist tradition, forty-nine is the number of days a soul wanders the earth for answers before the afterlife.

1

Dear Eun Ji.

Hello, hello, hello, my Eun Ji.

    You said you're doing well? We phoned yesterday, re-
member? Mommy got a little angry, but not at you. Mommy didn't take good care of things and had thoughts like,
"I've put you guys up in a very dirty place." If you lived with
Mommy, you wouldn't raise a dog and Eun Ji wouldn't be
alone at the house in Davis every day, right? Then, without
asking, you guys bought a *TV*. *Of course*, you could've done
that, but. *Anyway*, everything is fine. It's fine. After some
time passed, I realized, "They could've done that." Still, if
Aeson goes in and out of your room, the thought of my Eun
Ji's body, clothes, his dog hair sticking to everything, even

now it makes my heart ache. You can understand, right? Oh, my friend Gwi Won's daughter Jung Yeon (*finally*) got hired (*pass*) at KBS television studios. Starting next year, she will be an announcer and come on *TV*. Gwi Won was so hysterical she called me crying. Didn't it turn out well? For a year and a half, you don't know how many times Jung Yeon tested. It's a big, big deal. I'll have to thank God. Gwi Won had only been getting bad news as of late.

God is *fair*, you know. My Eun Ji is tired and lonely now, but you'll get good news too. You will go to the college you want, then *graduate* from college, get a *job*, and from here on, you'll only get lots and lots of good news. *Especially* in *college*, a *good boyfriend* will appear. Mommy's excited just thinking about it. Right?

Looks like you have exactly a week left of tests. This letter will probably *arrive* either a day before you test or just after you tested. When you feel a little better, if you want to talk to Mommy again, call me. I'll be waiting.

Tomorrow, your dad's second oldest brother's wife said she's coming over to play. We're going to the bathhouse together. You want to go, don't you?   *I know!*

You know the restaurant owner in the bathhouse? That woman said my Eun Ji is prettier than Jung Yeon. Mommy thinks so too.

My pretty Eun Ji. You know to live all you can and always boldly, right? Eun Ji must be *happy* so Mommy can be *happy*. When I *finish* this letter, I'll *pray* too. "God, *always* be with my Eun Ji and Chang Hyun. Please help my Eun Ji go to the *college* she wants." Like this, you know. I'll write again tomorrow. Bye. *Be happy.*

Mom
November 28, 2005

은지에게.

안녕 안녕 안녕 우리온지.
잘 지내고 있다며?
어제 전화 했잖아.
엄마가 좀 화가 났었거든, 너 한테가 아니고
엄마가 잘 보살피지 못하고
너네들을 너무 지저분한 곳에서 살게 하는구나' 하는
그런 생각이 들었어.
엄마랑 같이 살고 있었으면 개도 안키웠을 테고
은지가 매일 혼자 집에 있지도 않을테고, 그치?
너희들 마음대로 T.V도 사고
of cause 그럴수도 있지만.
Any way 다 괜찮아. 괜찮아.
시간이 지나니까 '그럴수도 있지' 그렇게 생각이 든다.
그래도 Aeson이 네방에 들락거리며
우리온지 몸에, 옷에 개털이 막 묻는다고 생각하면
지금도 속이 상해.
이해는 하지?
참. 귀원이 아줌마 딸 정연이 언니는 KBS 방송국에
드디어 (Finally) 합격 했다. (pass)
내년부터 아나운서가 되서 TV에 나올꺼야.
귀원이 아줌마가 너무 좋아서 울면서 전화 했더라.
정말 잘됐지?
1년 반을 시험은 몇 번을 봤는지 몰라.
정말 정말 축하할 일이야.
하느님께 감사 해야지
요즈음에 아줌마네 안좋은 일만 있었거든.

하나님은 fair 하시거든
우리 은지도 지금은 힘들고 외롭겠지만
곧 좋은 일도 생길꺼야.
원하는 대학에도 들어가고 또 대학 graduate
하고 job 가지고,
앞으로 좋은 일만 많이 많이 생길꺼야.
Specially, College 에 가서 good boy friend도
생기고,
엄마는 생각만 해도 즐겁다. 그치?
시험이 꼭 일주일 남았구나.
이 편지는 시험보기 하루전이나, 모레나서
도착 (arrive) 하겠다.
기분이 좀 좋아지고 엄마하고 또 얘기하고 싶으면
전화해. 기다릴게.
내일은 종현이네 큰 엄마가 놀러온데.
같이 찜질방에 갈거야.
너도 가고 싶지?　　I know!
찜질방에 식당 아줌마 있지?
그 아줌마가 우리 은지가 정연이 보다 이쁜대.
엄마 생각도 그래.
이쁜 은지.
열심히 살고 항상 씩씩해야 하는거 알지?
은지가 happy 해야 엄마도 happy 하고.
지금도 편지 finish 하면 pray 할께.
"하나님, always 우리 은지. 창현이랑 함께 하시고
우리은지 원하는 College 에 갈수 있도록 도와주세요"
이렇게 말야.
내일 또 쓸게. 안녕. be happy

mom
11/28/05

2

The present is the revenge of the past.

There is a Korean belief that you are born the parent of the one you hurt most. I was revenge when I was born in 1988 at O'Connor Hospital in San Jose, California. I was the reincarnation of somebody wronged, and no wonder I took out a chunk of my mother's body. It was late September. Not the average six pounder, I weighed ten pounds. The crown of my head split a fissure, and when my shoulders passed through, I nearly killed her. Broad, swathed in muscle and green veins, I was hairless except for the faint whiskers of eyebrows, and hungry, giving my mother and the doctor the impression of another boy.

That same day, at the hospital, my mother wiped her ripped parts and bussed to her job at the dry cleaners across town, passing her home—a six-hundred-square-foot unit at Sunnyhills, crowded apartments in Milpitas near sewage treatment ponds. It was her first month at the dry cleaners. She could not tell anyone that the stitches on her parts had opened. She hid in the bathroom to cry. Since her own mother had died young, she had looked after her siblings until she married. She had come to this country, taking her son—my brother—and following her husband and his elderly mother a year ago. Only her two brothers and her sister back home could comfort her. As she reached down where it hurt, her eyes swelled shut like the glazed ducks with baked eyes they hung out on hooks at the Lion Market.

When I was four, the doctor suspected I was a mute, a person who could not or would not speak, and no one could tell if I could read. Four and a half years and I had said nothing. Even so, at Berryessa flea market, at the Lion Market in Milpitas, at Yaohan Plaza in Fresno, my mother used my name like a fire poker to stoke me alive. The teacher urged her to put me in a school for children with learning disabilities. It was unthinkable to my mother, who chose to tutor me herself. She would have to stay home for longer. However, they needed extra money until my father graduated from school. In our apartment, she talked quietly since my father's mother napped on the floor pad in the same room. "Epper." Apple. She held it up. She took a bite of it. She drew a picture. A mother in pain may scold to the point of her own tears. When she had found out she was pregnant with me, my father and his mother urged her to lose the baby. She defied them for the chance that it might be a daughter. "Epper." Four doctor's visits, and she refused.

In 1993, at Santa Clara University, I was five and my brother nine when my heart broke with love for my mother, who was herself again, on the grass lawn, under the palm trees—she wore a red three-piece suit with sharp notch lapels, hair blown dry with a round brush. She stood a prisoner of her own light. A year before, my father, the youngest of six brothers and one sister, hauled around a crimson brick called the *Webster's New World Dictionary*. My father attended Santa Clara University for computer science and used the dictionary to learn English. My mother worked. He studied in the library. They decided together that his degree would be important one day. Six feet tall, 140 pounds, his shirts and pants were loose, yet he never complained. He said to me, in a calm voice shaped by his years in Korea's compulsory military service, "Some believe that if we're not smart like your mother and brother, we can't accomplish things. But we can if we are: one, funny, and two, humble." After he graduated and we took photographs under the palm trees, my father began to work, and my mother came home early—the resounding clamor of her unshackling. We moved out of Sunnyhills, fifteen miles to a house in Fremont, and my father fitted my mother with his class ring, *1993* engraved in gold, mounted with a red ruby.

~

Our family met fortune in the mid to late nineties. My father worked at a garage-sized networking company in Silicon Valley. He was a first hire and never broke from the company when they offered mere stock. Overnight, his one-dollar stock shot up to $280. My parents, who had prayed for years, were prepared. They poured two cups of barley tea and sold the house.

They bought a home atop a hill overlooking San Francisco Bay. They covered our kitchen in granite and marble, careful not to boast how the sun resided in our bay window, chandeliers above our dining table. Our tall cage where my parakeet, my mother's surprise for me on my thirteenth birthday, preened her white feathers. Chrysanthemums nodded inside their black vases and perfumed the house. The emerald lawn watered itself with pop-up sprinklers, splashing over our slab walkway, our brick foundation. Through the valley, the wind perpetually traveled with good news to us from our future.

I rushed to my parents' bedroom to say that I was home from school. Through their doors, their bedsheets moved like there was a whale under there. My father rolled over and cursed. Her hair, then her hand appeared. If I had never seen my mother and father hurt each other, I might never have known how they loved each other. They were doing what happy parents do.

~

If it was possible for my parents to be surprised, it happened when my father got a baffling job offer from an electronics company in Korea. I was fourteen years old. The company asked him to come to Seoul and head their advanced technology department. Maybe the company was exaggerating. Then they faxed him a three-year contract.

My parents quibbled over the offer without telling our neighbors. It was the kind of opportunity others might envy or criticize. Some were not ambitious; others might have signed up for longer considering how the company would finance our lives. Both position and pay left a knot of amazement on my parents' faces. They discussed the offer over sliced fruit, chewing seriously on yellow-ringed melons. The company would pay for college tuition. Two flights a year for visits. Should my parents move to Seoul, they would be sensible parents, well paid, confident with tall backs from splendored living. My father, a top-tier executive. My mother, reunited with her brothers and sister she had left behind seventeen years ago. Two luxury cars, a condo in a skyscraper, shopping sprees at the company-owned department store, new friends like themselves, could be theirs. They would have to live apart from their children, but only for three years. It was better to pay for your children than to stay with them. That was how it had always been. If the company had said four years, my parents would still have considered it. The years would pass quickly, unnoticeably. Their children could be proud of them. My parents could make new wrinkles around their eyes from smiling.

The offer changed my father. Wearing a slim polo, he asked my mother if he ought to try a livelier color. My mother had her brothers and sister on her mind. She wanted to see my father in salmon. Paired with light pants, the color made him look softer. My mother read his face—an age-old tradition. My father had a large nose, which meant good luck, but narrow-set eyes. His future would be lavish, albeit lonely, and she must protect him. If she wanted a bigger house, she would stay here. By square feet, the condo in Korea was smaller, so it would be easier to wipe down, my mother said, rubbing her shoulders, sore at the mention of cleaning. She packed her books, winter coats, and photo albums.

I would move in with my brother ninety-three miles north in Davis, on Oleander Place, a cul-de-sac off Covell Farms, in a one-story with a roof that sank slightly above the garage. The house was brown with white trim. The lawn, overgrown, midway to yellow. Two concrete steps led to a porch, a tin mailbox anchored by the door. From the driveway, the arch of a forty-foot ancient oak in the backyard, its knobby branches spread out, half covered the house in shade. The sidewalk dipped into a water ditch. The fire hydrant to the left was pure rust. The noise of traffic beyond a main road followed the signs of a college campus nearby. The house itself sat on a tilted stoop where it heaved forth a long-drawn-out sigh. They put me up to live with my brother and left the country in a hurry. My father flew with a briefcase so he could go to work as soon as he landed.

~

My first day, at fifteen, I awoke inside my old blanket, fooled into thinking that I was home. The room had a wooden desk, my same bed pushed against the wall, under a window facing the yard. There was a stucco ceiling and a mirrored closet. I looked for her in every room. When I could not find her, I felt as if I would die. In the kitchen, on the refrigerator, there was a paper note with her number. Her handwriting was evenly spaced the way she might arrange herself standing in a crowd.

I found my brother. I had watched him with our mother and father, but I never saw him in this city where he worked and went to school. If he walked into another room, I followed but stayed at the other end where he was both in my sight and far away. When he stalked into his own room, I suspected he hated to see me.

In elementary school, when my brother was ten, he picked me up at my bus stop. I had fallen asleep on board, so he passed the driver to drag me out by the loop of my knapsack. He was darker, a foot taller, fearless, and led me home seven blocks. One day, when my mother aimed a frying pan at my back after I had lied to her for the first time and she was pained to correct me, my brother stepped in front of it, splitting the handle; she moved away from my brother, who must have reminded her then of my father.

My brother slapped the house bills on the kitchen table. He looked at the clock hanging in the living room and waited for my mother to wake up. He took his phone into the yard and closed the sliding door behind him. From his voice, I guessed a pipe had burst. She would wire money as soon as the bank got back to them. It was difficult to move money, easier to move people. We waited for the water to be turned on. Opening the garage door, he got into his car and drove away.

Some say brothers cannot replace mothers and fathers. My mother called after he had left and said, "I'm not there, so your brother will take his anger out on you. Mommy knows all too well. Try to remember that he is mad at me, not you." The next morning, from the hall, I would look to see if my brother was in his room, and from his voice behind his door, hear what kind of day it would be. Other mornings, I found my brother hunched over his bedsheets, retreating into a small boy again, whose image would make any mother inconsolable to see it.

Outside, the oak shed its giant hairs. The wood siding invited termites to nest against the grain. I spent most days in my room after installing an interior lockset on my bedroom door. I twisted the rusted interior knob that worked in conjunction with pins and springs and tangs. Without a dead bolt on the door frame, the single cylindrical lock would have given out against a stampede of fists. But I fixated on the lock in that quiet house—privacy is the shadow of grief. Two or three times, I unlocked it to make sure it was locked to begin with. I stopped going to the new school regularly, missing a week or longer, though my brother did not know it. When he dropped me off, I walked to a nearby park and sat on a bench facing an empty gazebo for six hours before returning to the school where he picked me up, without a word, in his car. At the house, I slept for twelve hours or longer if I could, and come morning, I watched the sun come up like an egg cracked open underwater, its yolk rising with listlessness.

~

One spring day, after a year had passed in Davis, I was replacing the bedding of my parakeet's cage atop a table behind the sofa that separated Mieko from the living room. I had hugged Mieko's cage in the back seat of the car when I moved after standing firm that she would come with me. As I wiped down her tray and clipped fresh stalks of millet to her cage, as I did every week, Mieko looked down from her birch swing. My brother had also bought a Siberian husky he called Aeson. While I cleaned, Aeson watched from the living room. Normally, I waited longer to swap Mieko's tray, but my brother had complained about the smell before leaving the house. At a passing siren outside, Mieko, startled, flew out of her cage and, beating her clipped wings, crossed into the living room. Aeson, teeth first, snatched her up and escaped under the coffee table where I could not reach him. Crawling under, I kicked my legs. I heard him gnawing—a crackling. Her tiny screams. A louder crunch. How he crushed her, ground her down. Finally, I upended the table and seized Aeson by his neck, forcing my fingers into his jaws.

I had never seen a bird without bones. She lay flat on my palm like an envelope. When I was twelve, I had asked my mother for a parakeet. For a year, I tied a string to a plastic bag. It caught air, flying behind me like a bird. So little labor could bring so great a reward. I never knew a real bird was warm with tiny eyelashes, blue-gray eyelids. Violence felt wet in my palms. Her pellet-body punctured by dog teeth. Her feathers engulfed my hands. When my brother returned and saw what had happened, he must have been frightened because he shouted at me like I had never heard before, maintaining his cool, dry eyes. After he drove off in his car, I punched Aeson hard on the nose, but when I stumbled outside, Aeson still followed me, whimpering, and I was in no position to refuse company.

I buried Mieko in the backyard, at the fence, where I would often come to sit afterward. I wrapped her in a thin cloth and placed her inside a tin box with the millet she loved, in a hole a foot or two under the rightmost wooden panel. Children have no concept that every moment comes to end, but rather feel as though their suffering, at present, will last for an eternity. One small thing, taken away, was to feel the loss endlessly. I stole my brother's Lucky Strikes, left on the console table by the door. I took his lighter and retreated to the backyard. The living room sofa and rug would give up her feathers all month. I would clean, and it would not do anything. I curled up on the dirt and cried my heart out and smoked cigarettes. If anyone saw me, they might have wondered when everything had gone so wrong. They might have never known I would start to force up my food or starve myself. This city was famous for blue jays, seen almost everywhere—though it seemed inconsequential. Then I looked up at the oak tree, and there, a hundred birds came flying in on their fullest wingspan.

~

I almost saw a dead body once. I was ten or eleven, sitting beside my brother in the back seat of our sedan. My family was driving home after our monthly meeting at El Camino Real in Santa Clara, hosted each time by another Catholic family. The babies had gotten a taste of soju, kissing their parents on the mouth. We had pushed the lacquered foldout tables together for eight Korean Catholic families. The table settings: rice bowls on the left, soup bowls on the right. If we set the table oppositely, as we did for ancestral rites, then ghosts would devour our dinners. We tried not to disturb or refuse the dead.

Past eleven at night, our car exited the neighborhood, drove onto the on-ramp, and my parents began to let out their hateful thoughts about each other. At first, my mother folded her hands above her lap, then unbuckled herself to rise with the height of her voice.

My father's foot weighed heavy on the gas. His fist came down over the center console. The car veered off the shoulder of the freeway, then jolted back onto the road. A rosary hanging from the rearview mirror pedaled left and right. My brother cupped his hands over my ears.

My mother said, "I'll just die."

"No, I will," my father said.

"Why do you get to die?"

"Because I did all the work!"

From the passenger seat, my mother must have considered his words. In that second in the car, something closed inside her, and her face softened.

My mother opened the door until the light from outside filled the car. "You did all the work?" she asked calmly. "Then what am I?" Death must have seemed more approachable than her husband.

My father said, "Don't joke around—"

Suddenly, she jumped out.

Through the hinge of the door, her white skin passed slowly, the way she would go through the church door and into mass. She leaned out as though she might confess, beyond my field of vision.

I heard her body's density as she tumbled past me.

My father braked hard and the car lurched forward. The shocks and springs compressed, putting pressure on the joints, bushings, and bearings.

He pulled the car over, ran outside.

By the end of the month, she said cheerfully that she wasn't trying to kill herself. She changed her bandages before bed, rubbed on a paste for the burns on her right side. When churchgoers asked, she described outdoor concrete stairs, mimicked herself tumbling, and elbowed me to follow. Before long, she was walking normally.

My mother told me if she hadn't jumped, the whole car might have crashed. It would be a waste to see in the paper: dead parents and dead children, roasted inside a vehicle, separated into parts. She said to me, about the trouble with reincarnation, "What universe must God create for these souls to meet again and resolve their obligations?"

I never could jump out of a speeding car.

~

She began writing me letters from Korea in 2005. They had been gone for nineteen months. Once a week, a letter came. Her first was an airline postcard, addressing me as *Angela*. Her second was two pages in blue ink, describing the store where she had bought her pen. I did not know the Korean word for *fair*. But what we knew only in Korean or only in English, she tried to put together. I read the letter out loud to hear the sounds. Otherwise, I could not recognize the words and their shapes, filling the page, covering the creases.

In the letters, I heard her voice, closer than it felt over the phone. I read them in my room—sitting at the desk, standing in the doorway, lying on the bed. I folded the letter and slipped it into its envelope. I placed it on my nightstand. I kept her close. I read a letter once or twice. Moving my lips, I read it again. Each time, I hoped to see something new, a word that I had missed. When I put it away, a panic returned. I took out the same letter and, with no thought to what I had read before, started over.

Early one morning, the phone rang. Her voice sprinted into my ears. "I'm calling you because I miss you," she said. "Did you pick up because you miss me too?"

They had signed another contract with the company.

"My chest is tight," she said. "Will you hold bitter feelings against me?"

They would stay in Seoul for another two years. All together, they would be away for five years including the three years from the first contract. As we talked, my father renewed his work visa, but I said nothing. I put the phone back into its place on the wall next to the refrigerator. When my mother had first asked whether it was okay with me, I was fourteen and copied my brother. "I'm not a baby anymore," I had said to her, and now I huddled over the floor with the memory of all the words she had said to me then.

At the airport in San Francisco, on the day my mother had left the country, she had asked me again if I might come with her. She knew that I would be troubled growing up in another country but wanted me to come because she could not fathom how I would manage without her. She had to go, it was clear to her, but she said it would be difficult. "Do you know what happens after I'm gone?" she asked me. "You have to raise yourself with dignity. Your brother can be mean only when he is unsure of himself. But he loves you. We will look back at our time apart and laugh together and be sad, but we will have many stories. If you have no suffering, you have no story to tell—isn't it true?"

Standing there, she jokingly called me lazy, pointing to my long fingers as further proof. And I was gullible: my earlobes were so thin, words penetrated them easily. "When you age, wrinkles don't make you older. They make you look more like yourself," she warned me. "Everything comes to the surface eventually." Displays of celadon pottery, their pale green glaze, lit up inside their glass cases in the terminal. I did not cry in front of my mother, never having asked her to take me with her.

Before my mother's plane lifted off the airfield, the edges of her lips stretched taut into a smile. "If you're too nice to me, I won't be born again as Eun Ji's daughter," she said. "You must be my mommy, who's come back to make me happy."

~

Emboldened by impulse, I stole away to a playground, a half mile's walk from the Davis house, to freeze myself to death. In the dark, I heard Mieko's feet clasp the bars of her cage and Aeson barking past the road. In dreams of dying, a park and a body, frozen over, made a serene picture, but after three or four hours into the night I jolted awake in the grass, thrashing over the earth. There seemed no reason for me to live. Embarrassed, I trudged back over wet roads in a zigzag, aching. Though I did not expect a soul outside, a tunnel of light shone from the doorway of the house, where my brother stood, waiting, wrapped in a blanket. I ran toward his hand, outstretched with a mug of hot chocolate. He never asked

where I had been or why I had been gone for hours but offered hot cocoa he made from a mix he had bought on his trip
to the supermarket because he remembered the way it could
cheer me up, and he had been hoping to do just that, though
he did not know, always, the graceful way of doing so, but he
tried anyway, his very best, reminding me that we were not
stuck—we were liberated—and he understood at his young
age that he was all I had in this world, and only when he had
returned to his room and closed the door behind him did my
tears fall freely.

3

My beloved Eun Ji.

Today, your Auntie's visiting from Daejeon. She's buying a *coat* and wants Mommy to go with her. Her birthday passed, end of November, so she said her sons gave her money. She's probably riding the bus to Seoul now. Mommy will go along with her to pick something out, then make her buy me delicious food. Must be nice, right? I know. Mommy has it so good. For the 1 year and 5 months I have left, I've got to have fun with my big sister.

    Oh, do you know Auntie's name?

    Auntie's name is Lee Jeong Lim.

    Auntie is 58 *years old*. 10 years older than Mommy.

    Big Uncle is Lee Min Seung.

Little Uncle is Lee Kyo Seung.

Their ages are 50 *years old* and 44 *years old*.

Didn't know, did you? It's not important, but at least, you should know their names. Right?

Mommy is so thankful. Although (*even if*) I live apart from you guys, I'm also spending time together with my family (*brothers, sister*) for a couple years, so I'm very grateful. However, many times, I don't see them even once a month.

For Auntie, I feel sorry that she doesn't have a daughter, and she must get jealous (*envy*) because I have my Eun Ji. (Should I tease her?)

These days, what're you up to? The weather's cold and it's rainy, isn't it? Pay attention to your health, and times like these, read a bunch of good books. Things you don't know, things you can't *experience*, all of it lies inside of books.

A while ago (*a few months ago*), Mommy read a book written by a Japanese author called, "How to Age with Grace." Though I can't do everything in the book as well, I want to live as a good person and age with grace. Eun Ji will help me, won't you? How could you help me, you ask? Hm ~ It's easy and it's hard, too. Don't give Mommy heartaches. Soothe her to keep her from anger or shouting. When Mommy has bad thoughts, or acts unfairly, tell me that I shouldn't do that. How about it? You'll do it for me, won't you? Thank you.

Mommy, too, will make sure, through *cooperation*, that Eun Ji goes on living as a healthy, brave, and kind-hearted person. This next time, I want to be born as Eun Ji's Mommy again to live and become a better Mommy. Or should I be born as Eun Ji's daughter? If you give birth to me as a pretty and nice person, then I can agree to it? Just thinking about it cracks me up.

Well, babies should give heartaches and be exhausting so that Mommies can grow. And learn. Isn't that right? Now, there are 10 *days* left. I miss you. And I love you so much.

Mom
December 9, 2005

사랑하는 은지야.

오늘은 대전에서 이모가 올거야.
Coat 사는데 엄마랑 같이 가자 했대.
11월 말에 생일 이있는데 아빠 둘이 돈 줬대.
그래서 지금 고속버스 타고 오고 있을거야.
엄마는 따라 다니면서 골라주고 맛있는거 사달래야지.
좋겠지?
그래. 엄마 너무 좋아.
이제 1년 5개월 남았는데 언니하고 잘 지내야지.
참,
너 이모 이름 알아?
이모 이름은 이 정림 이야.
이모 나이는 58 years old 고.
엄마보다 10산 많다.
큰 삼촌은 이 민승
작은 삼촌은 이 교승 이고
나이는 50 years old, 44 years old 야.
몰랐었지?
중요한 건 아니지만 이름정도는 알아야지. 그치?
엄마는 참 감사하다.
비록 (even if) 너희들하고 헤어져 살고 있지만
대신 내 형제 (brothers, sisters)들과
몇년이라도 같이 지낼 수 있게되서 너무 감사해.
그래도 한달에 한번도 못 만날때도 많아.
이모는 딸이 없어서 불쌍하고.
엄마가 우리은지 있는게 너무 부러운 (envy)가봐.
(약올려 줄까?)

요즘은 뭐 하고 지내?
날씨도 춥고 비도 오지?
건강에 신경 쓰고 이럴때 좋은 책도 많이 읽어.
내가 모르는거, 경험하지 못하는거, 모두
책속에 있어. experience
엄마는 얼마전에 (few months ago) '아름답게
늙는법' 이란 일본사람이 쓴 책을 읽었어.
책에 있는대로 다 잘 할 수는 없지만
좋은 사람으로 살다가 아름다운 모습으로 늙고싶어.
은지가 도와 줄거지?
어떻게 해야 하느냐구?
음 ~ 쉽기도 하고 어렵기도 해.
엄마 속상하지 않게 해주고,
화내고 소리지르지 않게 달래주고,
엄마가 나쁜생각, 옳지 않은일 하면 말려주고,
그러면 안된다고 말해주고,
어때? 해줄거지? 그마워.
엄마도 은지가 건강하고 씩씩하게 고운 사람으로
살아 갈 수 있도록 Cooperation 할께.
엄마는 이 다음에도 은지 엄마로 태어나서 살면서
좀더 좋은 엄마가 되고 싶어.
아님, 은지 딸로 태어날까?
이쁘고 착한사람으로 낳아 주면 그렇게 할까?
생각만 해도 재미있고 좋다.
하긴, 자식이 속도 좀 썩이고 힘들게 해야
엄마들이 자라는거야. 배우기도 하고, 맞지?
이제 10 days 남았다.
보고싶어. 그리고 많이 사랑해

Mom
12/09/05

4

In the summer after high school, my flight had landed in Incheon on a late afternoon, and I arrived in Bundang, Seoul to see my mother. I visited her in the winter and summer on flights covered by the contract. We had been living apart almost two years when she told me that our fortune had grown with my father at his company. They had moved from one side of the Tancheon River to the other. There were no telephone cables overground, only a clean cityscape with silk-tie shops, garden cafés, and department stores. It was nothing like my trips to other parts of the country when I was a child, and people took *banchan* to their neighbors, who beamed behind the sliding clothbound doors of tightly spaced houses shouldering the dirt roads that climbed the sky.

I got out in front of a chrome skyscraper surrounded by a six-foot pale rock wall and two iron security gates for cars to come and go. Beyond the gates, a guard at his post eyed me, raised his hand, and signaled another guard across the garage to let me in. The gates opened toward me. In the distance, at the mouth of the skyscraper, a silhouette of a woman appeared. She bowed to the guards who received her. From her palms, she offered tangerines and dried squid for their break time, and they apologized for accepting. She was as thoughtful as their own mothers.

My mother embraced me and, in a whisper, instructed me to bow in greeting to the guards. "They're hardworking and courteous." She patted my shoulder because I had grown taller. "Grandfathers who're the first and last to bow to our guests." She twirled around for me in her white crepe blouse and pearl drop earrings. Her face glossy with serum, she said, "I haven't dressed up like this since my mommy dressed me as a little girl." She had done it for me. She wanted to look pretty—wasn't she?

"What's wrong with you?" my mother asked, then reminded me that flights could make anyone feel unlike themselves.

She ushered me into the lobby, waving toward the guards, who bowed uniformly, showing the tops of their heads. Behind the doorman's desk, she checked a silver-plated slot.

"You don't have a mailbox?" I asked her.

"This *is* my mailbox." She laughed and took me up on the elevator. The elevator was paneled in mirrors. Her profile stepped out onto the eighteenth floor. To open a metal door, she entered a six-digit passcode. "The passcode is your birthday," she said.

~

The world opened to pure white ceilings and rooms. The east wall of her living room was a tremendous sheet of glass overlooking the city. Her kitchen had foldable cupboards like origami, springing open then shutting flush against the boards. One unfolded five feet to reveal a cubby with gifts of wine and pears, then concealed itself again. Another contained a circular microwave. "I couldn't wait for you to see all of our new stuff," she said, flashing two car keys, as if she had gotten them yesterday, and credit cards gifted by the company for the department store with its green rooftop that was visible from where we stood.

"Your brother called me." She pouted and dropped her head. "I *baby-treat* him too much. I have to stop nagging him and let him go. I have to change my thinking." He had visited her before, but after once or twice, he stopped.

"He was too busy to come," I answered.

"Oh," she said. "I've been buying this and that, collecting souvenirs. Look at these tiny spoons. I have this rabbit and I call her Eun Ji." She held up a stuffed doll by the ears and showed it to me. "Sometimes she doesn't listen to me. I keep her in your room."

"You keep it in my room?"

"It's across the hall."

Looking inside, I saw socks flipped at the ankles on the nightstand, as if the night before, I might have thrown them to the floor. Cleaning, she would have picked them up.

She frowned. "When I miss you, I lie on this bed until your dad gets home."

"When does he get home?"

"Maybe eleven," she said. "Your poor dad hates working in this country."

It was as we stood over my bed, its flower bedsheets and department-store blankets, that she asked me if I needed her to come back. Knowing that they had already signed on to stay for another two years, that my father's contract had been extended owing to his good work, I did not know why she asked. Her words had not yet settled when she reassured me that by the time she came back, I would have forgotten how I had missed her. "You tell the kind and patient person," she said, "to be more kind and patient. That's why my Eun Ji will live the hardest life."

My mother fussed over my clothes. Sniffing, she told me to throw them off because they were rotten. Then she cursed my patchy skin; of course I was sick so often. After a scrub at the bathhouse, she said quickly, cradling my head against her shoulder, my dead layers would fall away to show the smooth and clean, boiled-egg texture underneath. "A few weeks with me," she said, "and you'll look and feel differently than you do now."

~

My mother's regular department store was thirty-two floors tall. Thirty-two floors of luxury goods, each department happy to accept her credit cards gifted by the company. Beyond the department store's three golden rotating entrance doors were playrooms, cafés, movie theaters, designer stores, and wedding halls. The floors above were divided into beauty, clothing, home, electronics, and books. In the basement, the discount and returns section of the store, paper *won* passed between shoppers and clerks. Nearby, nuptials from the hall; gunfire from the cinema.

My mother told me to call the girls working the clothing floor *sisters*. They greeted my mother with high, zesty voices ringing around the endless corners. The girls wore navy blue suit jackets with stiff collars and navy blue skirts and heels. Every hair was waxed, combed into a bun; every lip a bright red. The girls wore clean white gloves to handle expensive items. They turned their wrists in dove-winged gestures to direct my mother ahead, offering her a reduced price on a "hot item" bag and complimentary face masks. They said to her, "Hello again, dear customer" and "Please ask us anything" and "Come in, take your time" and "Welcome to our store" and "We have everything you're looking for."

I barely stood on both feet, instead shifting my weight from one to the other, and I slouched. When the girls bowed to me, their mouths could not hide their apprehension at my wrestling shoes and my hoodie. They recognized me as a wealthy daughter, who studied abroad and wore torn jeans and spoke English.

I stared into the shop. Shiny displays of black dresses; cardigans for summer modesty. A feeling arose within me: I loved this place and its fineness. My heart landed on one lovely thing, then another. White scalloped tops on wooden hangers. Chiffon ruffle blouses on mannequins. Cream leather jackets with silver zippers. Meanwhile, my mother stormed through the shop as if it were a street market.

My fingertips grazed a shark's-tooth-patterned coat. Teal and black pulsated through the coat's body, all of it lined in silk. The collar was stiff and structured. The sleeves widened at the bottom—a touch of whimsy.

The shopgirl came up to me. Grinning, she must have believed she had caught a fish—not the mother but her daughter. Two inches shorter than me with an uncomplicated beauty, she was better suited for the coat than I was. Folding her gloved hands at her waist, she said, "The color's unique. It's eye-catching, don't you think?"

"Thank you, sister. It's on sale," I said to help her cause.

"Because it's a coat from this past winter." She raised the coat to eye level in front of us. "It's too attractive to pass up, both the coat and the price."

"It's bold, sister," I said, keeping up with her formality.

"You can't not look at it, can you?" She showed the back of the coat. "If no one bought it, I wanted it for myself. I admired it like a lover, and here you've come to take it."

"Really?" I asked.

"I'm jealous," she said, and ran her fingers along the seam. "The coat stands out and so do you. You're meant for each other."

I bowed, prepared to leave her department. But my mother, far ahead on the walkway, spun around to face me. Retracing her steps, she entered the section. The girl kept her back to my mother, seemingly ignoring her, but addressing me clearly so that she could hear. "You look so young, and your Korean sounds delicate," she said to me. "What's your name?"

My mother laughed. "This is my daughter."

The girl held her hands higher on her waist. "She looks just like you, ma'am."

"Really, is that true?" my mother asked. "Of course, it makes me happy."

"She's not like the girls here," she said. "Was she born here?"

"My daughter was born in America—it keeps her innocent."

"Oh, I can see it," the girl said. "She must have no bad thoughts at all."

My mother clapped once. "If she got lost here, she'd be gone forever!"

The girl said, "You know how they say everything—"

"Everything comes to the surface eventually!"

My mother scrutinized the coat. She shook it out, as if it was laundry fresh from the dryer. "Only my daughter would pick this one." She was using her mother wit for a bargain, and my job was to notice it.

"Your daughter has good taste," the girl said in reply.

"This looks cheap, like wholesale," my mother said. "What's the original price?"

The girl presented the tag with two hands.

My mother looked impressed. "This ratty old thing?"

"It's one of a kind," the girl said to her. "Hand-sewn."

My mother scoured for loose threads and a discount.

"Let's go," I said to my mother, who was unaware of the other shoppers and their glances our way. "I don't need it, sister. Thank you—"

My mother's nails pinched my forearm. "Hold on," she said to me. "Give me a second."

The next words mattered. The girl said to her, "Your daughter is so lucky to have a mother like you."

My mother nodded approvingly. "Let's do a bigger cut off the price—"

"Oh, I'm a shopgirl," she said. "You know I can't haggle like that—"

"Whatever you can, I'll give you cash—"

"Please, don't fuss. This isn't a place for that—"

"Tell me the price again?" My mother counted new, clean bills. "I'll come back to your shop again with my friends next week, and we'll each buy something."

The girl sighed. "Are you sure?"

"Mmm hmm."

"Okay, fine," she said. "Since you're a *special* customer."

"I won't forget it," my mother said to her.

The girl wrapped the coat in a bag. "I can't spit on a smiling face."

"Yes, you've made us smile." My mother eased up and took the girl's hand. "You're so smart and fast. You're a good girl. You don't say too much, you don't give too much."

The sale finished, the girl's shoulders relaxed. She pulled me to her side, as though we were friends now holding hands. This was how it must feel to have a sister. "Your daughter speaks Korean?" she asked my mother. "She speaks both, it's impressive."

"This," my mother said, raising the bag with the coat, "is the most expensive thing I ever bought her. She doesn't live in California like I do here. It's hard to take money and move it across the world. It's easier to move people."

"Then your daughter should wear it out."

My mother nodded gratefully as the girl swapped my hoodie for the coat. She guided me into the sleeves, one after the other, then gave me a tie to pull my hair back.

"How is it?" the girl asked me. "Do you feel refreshed?"

"Oh, oh, she's starting to look like me," my mother said. "Do you see?"

"It's her eyes," the girl said. "Your daughter has the best of both. She'll grow up to have a glamorous figure, like an American. When she came in today, I could tell she was different. She has so much ki. You can't help but notice. The girls are curious. They were saying, 'How mysterious!' 'How quiet, solemn, dark-skinned. Can she be so young?'"

"It's my fault." My mother took the bag with the hoodie, tucked it under her arm. "It's all my doing. I made her suffer too much. I didn't know what to give her, so I gave her pain. She's lovely, isn't she?"

"She is pure," the girl comforted her.

"You've suffered too," my mother said to her. "Whose poor daughter are you?"

"My parents are missionaries," she said. "I'll marry and move into my husband's house to live with his parents the day before my waist thickens but no sooner."

My mother patted her head. "You have a lucky forehead. You'll have many suitors. And you're right to wait. Nobody loves you like your mother and father. Not your husband, and not your children. While your parents are alive, eat as much of their love as you can, so it can sustain you for the rest of your life."

In the shop's oval mirror, the coat embraced me.

"What a reduction," the girl said to me. "You're lucky to have a mother like her."

My mother said, "There was one woman, prettier than anyone. It was my own mother. Back in the old days, you couldn't hide beauty. In those plain huts, dirt roads, can you imagine how she stood out? It was impossible to live in the countryside. She died young and tragically." My mother squeezed my hand in hers. "I was a little girl when she died, and she left me to live without her."

~

For an early dinner, we hunted for barbecued duck. My mother drove outside the city, past a construction site, onto an uphill road, through a forest of pale-limbed trees with thin branches that pointed to the sky. Where the road narrowed, we came to a hidden driveway that led to a two-story restaurant on wooden stilts.

The duck was presented in neat rows of thin slices, sunning on our floor table. Pointing to the new coat I was wearing, my mother would not let me cook. Using metal chopsticks, she rested a slice over the grill, charred it on each side, dipped the cooked slice into a sweet mustard, and fed it to me. Tender, rich, and smoky. Driving here no longer seemed out of the way. Our iced coffees were ten dollars each.

"Slow down," my mother said. "You're going to choke."

"Let's order more," I said, feeling more awake. "More mustard too."

"Are you starving yourself at home?"

I did not tell her that I ate cookies, chips, and cereal out of the cupboards. Even as I felt pain in my stomach, I wanted more. The first time I had made myself throw up, at the age of sixteen, I had found relief in my Davis bathroom. From then on it was normal for me to go on eating, then undo what I had done. There were tooth marks on my knuckles. My jaw was swollen.

For all I knew, I was the only person in the world forcing up my food. Only I could feel the bones of my feet in my shoes; only I saw my nails feather at the tips and felt scared when I noticed a piece of my throat, a strip of flesh, sinking to the bottom of the toilet bowl. I swore that I would not do it while staying with my mother.

The waitress kneeled at our table and hugged me, causing my chopsticks to clatter to the floor. She removed new ones from her apron, set them on the table, and said, "I feel like I'm seeing a ghost. I've listened to your mother talk about you for hours. She had to bring you out here just to prove to me that you were real. She didn't pay you, did she?"

The waitress, who looked to be in her forties, had wrinkles around her mouth. Women with sons have this face, my mother once told me. While you can fight with your daughter, you must bite your tongue in front of your son.

She scooted right next to me and warned me about my mother's friends, or the wives of my father's friends. "Those people, they'll see a girl like you, take you to a place like this, then get you drunk and bring you home to one of their mansions, and they'll trap you and lock you in a room with one of their lonely sons!"

My mother laughed. She used to be a waitress and must often have found herself friendlier with waitstaff than she did with my father's friends and their wives. "Young women," she said, "are more valuable than men these days."

"God," the waitress said, slapping the floor. "They'd be overjoyed to get her pregnant and then force her to marry their sons. Then, they'd get a daughter *and* a grandchild. A daughter to order around, a grandchild to show off."

"It wasn't always like that," said my mother.

"Praise the Lord," said the waitress.

"Do you like her new coat?" my mother asked her.

"It's true what they say," the waitress said to me. "Your clothes are your wings."

The waitress shifted from a kneel into a squat, dug into her back pocket, and slid an envelope across the floor. My mother bowed to her, gathered the envelope, and transferred it into a larger envelope inside her purse.

"My husband's friend's wife wants to meet my daughter tonight," my mother said. They both acted as though the envelope had not passed between them. "She's buying us barbecued eel. That woman has an elevator in her house!"

The waitress clapped her hands. "What a lonely woman to beg!"

"Pity is the path to mutuality," said my mother.

"Oh, screw pity. She has an elevator!"

~

My mother drove to her regular bathhouse, which we entered through a parking garage so far underground that you could feel the air cooling. We emerged from an elevator. She paid at the front desk. The woman set out two sets of shirts and shorts to sweat in, and towels. We rinsed in the showers. We soaked inside the pools. The steam rose, filigree above our shoulders in the shape of white swans. On spa tables, our bodies were scrubbed raw and rolls of dead skin collected beneath us.

I asked my mother about the envelope. My mother's friends saved for big purchases by adding each month to a pot, and one of them received the *gye* payout on a rotating basis. The women had chosen my mother to be their collector and distributor. She was good with numbers in her head at the market.

Her eyes were closed. "With my payout?" she asked me. "I send it to my brothers. I left you and your brother to come here and be with my family. But I don't know how their lives can be so difficult. How can they live so poorly? How can I ask your dad for money to help my brothers? My brothers are too proud." She took a towel and put it over her face. Through the cloth, she said, "So, I send my brothers' wives bags of rice. I give envelopes of money to their children. If our own mother hadn't died so young, maybe things would've been different. How can they lead such unfortunate lives?"

Our bodies were flipped onto our sides and the scrubbing resumed.

"My brothers were so handsome," she said, suddenly. "When I was in school, my friends chased my brothers. They were famous for their elegant eyes and strong features. As they got older, their faces changed. Now they look tired, weighed down. But when they're sleeping, all their worries leave their face, and they look young again."

"Are you okay?" I asked.

"I don't know why I'm crying," she said to me. "I don't know—"

"Who cares, you feel bad," I said.

"Listen to you," she said, sharply. "Koreans don't say 'who cares' to their mothers. One day, you'll have a daughter who treats you like you treat me."

We rinsed ourselves with ginseng body wash. Then, we headed to the outside main room with an ondol-heated floor in our shirts and shorts. We entered the clay room and left after a short time. We crawled into a dome-shaped stone sauna and sat on the floor. My mother apologized. "You're old enough to be my friend," she said.

"You have a lot of friends."

She said, "My friend from college, Gwi Won. We tried to be news anchors."

"News anchors?" I asked. "You never talked about it."

"Because you see me *now*, but if you saw me *then*, I was good, really." She wiped her sweat off. She motioned for me to do the same. "My mother was good at everything."

"Did you pass the audition?"

"I did," my mother said, "but Gwi Won didn't."

"And you became a news anchor?"

"No, Gwi Won lied. She told me I didn't pass either."

"What?" I said. "That makes no sense."

"My dad never let me out of the house. Gwi Won checked the results for us and said that we didn't make it. The broadcast-ing station was waiting. They called me to tell me they couldn't wait any longer. After a month, they had hired somebody else."

"Are you still friends with her?" I asked.

"I am," she said. "Two persimmons, getting old."

"What—why?"

"Let's drink something delicious," my mother said.

She charged my sweet rice drink to her tab. The ice was refreshing in the hot rooms. I kept one cube under my tongue. My mother led me into the charcoal room. She poured water over the heated rocks in the corner. We shuffled onto the floor and sat facing one another.

"You know Gwi Won? The one who lies?" my mother said after a silence. "I already told you that her daughter is a news anchor. Do you remember? We see her on TV. She has short hair and a button nose. She's prettier in person. We watch her on variety shows and news broadcasts. I go to see Gwi Won and we record them together. One time, this was in front of my friends, I asked if she thought my daughter could pass for a news anchor. Gwi Won said my daughter's face is too big for the screen. Your face needs to fit inside a CD disc to look good on television. From your forehead to your chin."

I measured my face with my palm for the first time.

"How many people can cover their face with a disc?" she asked.

"Maybe you shouldn't be friends."

"You think so?"

I nodded, but she disagreed.

"God is fair," she said, and clasped our hands together. "Gwi Won had a stroke. Half her face melted off and it sags down past her chin. When she smiles, it bends into a sneer. You see, God is vengeful, so we don't have to be."

~

At the end of our time at the bathhouse, I put on my coat and followed my mother into the parking garage where she fed her ticket into a machine. We drove home in silence. After we got out of the car, we went for a walk around the Tancheon.

I worried about whether I ought to take off my coat or wear it casually on the walking path along the river. I feared my mother might admire me wearing it and express her satisfaction. But I felt it would be worse to put the coat away. When I asked my mother about her own mother, she said, "How fun would it have been if my mother was here with us? We would scrub each other's backs, like baby monkeys sitting in a neat row."

"She would be the most beautiful."

My mother laughed. "She had a big face, but it was a beautiful face. And she'd never let you leave the department store with just one coat. She would've bought you a dozen." Then she tugged my sleeve. "If you ever get sick of wearing this, give it to me. I'll save it for you, and one day, you'll think about it and ask me for it. You'll say, 'Oh, that coat from *then*!' When you put it on, you'll feel like you do now."

"I feel refreshed," I said. "Do I remind you of her?"

"Your brother tells me that you're strong and you never cry." My mother smiled sadly. "You know how my mother is dead? Do you think she feels lonely?"

5

Hello? Eun Ji,

I was so happy after we talked on the phone this morning. Seemed like you were in a better mood, too. Thank you for singing my favorite song for me. I nearly cried. Sing for me again next time. I love to hear Eun Ji's voice any time.

Sure, it's not easy for a person to live their life. For adults or babies, it's all the same. Our feelings are different (because our thoughts are different). Because our wants are different. Actually, everyone's the same. Our sadness, sometimes, our joys. Our (*hopelessness, despair*). Mommy's like that, too. When you're my age, you think you'll outgrow everything, but it's not true. Every day, my thoughts change, and I lose *control*.

However, Eun Ji, our lives, being given to us, is the most precious time. Of course, the ups and downs go together, but let's not (*waste*) any moment not feeling happy (not being *happy*). You know the American president John F. Kennedy? That person said this: "When you lose your things, you're not losing much. When you lose (*trust*), you're losing a lot. When you lose (*courage*), you're losing everything." What do you think? These are very good words, aren't they?

Promise (*confirm*) and say it to yourself (*myself*) constantly. If anyone asks for help, be (*willing to*) reach out your hand. If anyone needs guidance, you do so earnestly (*honesty*).

You know penguins? Penguins support each other with *order, discipline*. Mommy read this in a book, and she will *copy* it word for word:

> When penguins in (*the South Pole*) endure
> frigid (very cold) winds, they huddle tightly
> together with their body heat. The penguins
> on the side with raging winds will alternate
> with the penguins in the back where there
> is almost no wind. The penguins all abide
> by this *rule*. If some penguins try to remain
> only in the back, then it will be difficult for
> them to survive themselves.

Do you understand? Working together, you are much stronger. You can't only help others either. When you're having a hard time, tell somebody. If you want to throw a tantrum, you should try it. I'm not sure what to say to help Eun Ji, but from Mommy's point of view, you're doing very, very well. Eun Ji has grown to be successful and goodhearted, more than what Mommy hoped for. Everything is a process. Everything passes . . . Let's always try to live with a bright, beaming heart. Mommy, too. Eun Ji, too.

I love you, my Eun Ji. Your songs, thank you so very much for them.   Bye.

Mom
January 18, 2006

안녕? 은지

아침에 통화하고 나서 너무 기뻤어.

기분이 많이 좋아진 듯 했고,

특히 엄마가 좋아하는 노래를 불러줘서 너무 고마워

눈물이 날 뻔 했어.

다음이 또 불러줘.

은지 목소리는 언제 들어도 좋아.

그래,

사람이 산다는게 쉽지 않아.

어른이나 아이나, 다 똑같애.

서로 감정이 다르고, (생각이 다르니까)

원하는게 다르니까 그렇지. 사실은 누구나 다 같애.

때로 슬프고, 즐겁고. 절망하고, (hopelessness, despair)

엄마도 그래. 이 나이쯤 되면 모든것에서

벗어 났을것 같은데 그게 아냐.

매일 매일 생각이 변하고 Control이 안되고 그렇지.

하지만 은지야.

우리의 인생은 하느님이 주신 무척 소중한 시간이란다.

물론 슬픔도 기쁨도 다 함께 해야 하지만

불행 (happy 하지 않은것)을 느끼는데 시간을

낭비 (waste) 하지 말자.

미국 대통령 존F 케네디 알지?

그 사람이 이런말을 했어.

'물건을 잃으면 작게 잃는 것이고, 신용 (trust)을

잃으면 크게 잃는 것이다. 용기를 (courage) 잃으면

모든것을 잃는 것이다.'

어때?

정말 좋은 말이지?

늘 스스로에게 (myself) 말해주고 다짐하는거지.
그렇다고 conform 하는것

누군가가 도와 달라고 하면 기꺼이 (willing to)
손을 내밀어 힘이 돼주고,

누군가의 도움이 필요하면 정직하게 말하는거야.
honesty

펭귄 알지? 펭귄들도 서로 도와주고 질서를 지킨다.
order, discipline

엄마가 책에서 읽은건데 그대로 copy 할게.
'남극 (the south pole) 펭귄은 매서운 바람이 불면
아주 추운

옹기종기 모여 서로 온기를 나눈다. 바람이 몰아치는
쪽에 있던 펭귄은, 잠시 뒤 바람이 거의 들지 않는
뒤쪽으로 옮긴다. 이때 다른 펭귄이 나와 바람에
맞서는데 이 rule을 모두 지킨다. 늘 뒤쪽에만
있으려 하면 자기도 살아남기 어렵다'

이해가 되니?
서로서로 도와주고 힘이 되줘야 된다는 건데.
늘 다른 사람만 도와주지 말고 너도 힘들면
힘들다고 말해. 꾀 부리고 싶으면 그렇게도 해보고.
어떤 말을 해야 은지한테 도움이 되지는 모르겠지만
엄마가 온기 은지는 너무너무 잘하고 있어.
엄마가 생각한것 보다 훨씬 훌륭하고 좋은사람으로
커가고 있는것 같아.
모든건 과정이야, 지나가는 거고 ...
항상 밝은 마음으로 살도록 애써보자. 엄마도, 은지도.
사랑해 우리은지.
노래. 정말 정말 고마웠어. 안녕
mom
2006. 1. 18

6

Daejeon 1972, 140 kilometers south of Seoul: my grandmother Jun, thirty-two, sewed skirts for her fourteen-year-
old daughter, my mother, on a seat at the Western table
in her two-story home. Jun crossed her knees, fluffing her
chiffon dress, which she paired with rich green indoor slippers. Her permed curls framed her slender ears. Jun cut her
daughter's skirts an inch too short on purpose. She felt an-
tagonistic about the police's use of measuring tapes to moni-
tor dress lengths. Jun and her husband were distinguished
by their wealth. Her life was blessed enough that the police
did not bother her or her daughter about their dresses.

Her daughter, starting middle school, hated to stand
out against the village roads, the thatch-roofed houses, the
dried straw packing the waterspouts during long windless

summers. Her daughter preferred plain cotton dresses that covered her legs and ankles, same as the villagers who dipped their hands into clay jars of fermented bean paste. Jun's teeth were too straight for her daughter, Jun's rings, too many, and Jun's mermaid silhouette embarrassed her.

The students at her daughter's school waggled their tongues at Jun's showiness, her sashaying on stilettos when she was already taller than her husband—her contempt for tradition. Jun refused kimchi over rice, good for digestion, and instead broiled fatty pork for school meetings and ladled thick white broth for her daughter's teachers and boasted that her daughter, who'd joined the journalism club, had won a poetry award. "My daughter," she said, "loves poetry."

Jun was grateful that her daughter had no memories of the occupation and war, of girls padding their robes for warmth, or of the others who had vanished. If Jun herself had not caught typhoid, she would have vanished too. Her daughter was born into industrial development, vaccinations, winding freeways, and television. She was born into a spirited country while Jun had waited to feel anything in her heart of her own.

Village husbands and boys were desirous of Jun. The village had thought this might change in time. But after Jun gave birth, she slimmed down while her curves stayed put. When she strutted to the market in a tight bodysuit with a fur collar, accentuating her serpentine shape, the other mothers covered their boys' eyes. The other mothers swore Jun could steal the purity so tediously reinstated after the enslavement of their women. The only thing they liked about her was her prosperous husband.

Stout and muscular, her husband, Lee, was generous with his money. Lee lent without interest and never raised his voice in a quarrel. Owing to his prosperity and high standing, no man sought out his wife in any serious manner, even when he traveled for work. Under his woven coat, his broad arms flexed, bearing back against any threat to his peace. He, a countryman, valued peace over everything. Everything but other women.

Swimming fish was tastier than a caught one.

For other men, Jun was swimming fish. But for her husband, Jun had long been caught. After some years living faithfully with her as husband and wife, Lee returned to his mistresses. He could afford to have them.

One night, Lee got home past the hour agreed upon with Jun. He slipped out of his gray wool suit into his pajamas, as if changing from one man into another.

Jun gleaned, from the way Lee tugged his arms out of each sleeve, that he had arrived from the bosom of a mistress. Somebody had dressed him in a hurry before he had entered their gates. Perhaps it was earlier, as early as this morning; second breakfast at a hotel or an apartment by the bund. Could he buy a house for his mistress? Carry her, pale legs swinging, into a bath larger than their own? Why did he not gorge on Jun's braised short ribs? Had he already taken dinner? Jun was an accomplished seamstress, a home cook, an opera singer, a natural beauty. Jun and Lee had only two sons and one daughter, but when Lee had introduced a girl, older than their eldest, birthed by a nameless woman, Jun had quietly adopted the girl with Lee's square features, his hooded eyes, and loved her. All the while, this other woman, did she tear his clothes, sobbing and moaning, bereaving him of energy, then send him back to Jun for mending, for boiled young chicken and ginseng to rejuvenate him? Then why not die?

~

Jun could not die because she had children, everybody knew. Jun looked for scissors, a sharp-edged pair in her wooden vanity with her combs, and as wives in love sometimes do, she cut the price tags off her husband's new suit jacket before she hung it for him on a wire hanger without a word. Lee was a busy man, made busier by his mistresses.

Jun could not hide her jealousy any longer, even if she feared driving him away. She accused Lee at the market when his handshake lingered with a woman hocking anchovies. Anchovies! "Finally," she said, "I know that I am capable of murder." The villagers could not make sense of Jun's whole-bodied jealousy. Their lack of understanding was bothersome; their righteousness, cruel. The other women, especially the wives, chastised her. If Jun lamented among vintage coats and blue opals and well-fed children inside a two-story brick house, what more could she desire?

"Because I love him," Jun said, sounding like a child.

~

Her daughter agreed with the other mothers even if, no, *because* she had witnessed from behind one of their home's crafted doors, looking into her mother's bedroom, Jun hugging herself on the floor. On an impulse, Jun seized her ankles and rocked and wailed pitifully, scolding herself against the trenchant silence of her polished home and her empty bedroom. Who says love that is painful is not love?

Midyear, Jun got into the medicine drawer, swallowed a handful of pills, as if taking down her existence whole. Yet she lived because her existence was spiky and stubborn.

The following year, after drinking her evening barley tea, Jun used the kitchen knife to open her arms. Her arms were two sausages torn from their skin.

Six months afterward, Jun shopped for a new dress shirt for Lee and set it atop their dresser for him to wear the next morning before returning to her room to crank up the gas from the reserve tank and fall asleep.

Each time, Jun survived.

~

Jun woke up in the hospital after the gas tank incident. There were village dogs crossing the road outside her window. Young men, released from their military duties, had changed into school uniforms. Wearing black caps, they marched in procession in black shoes. The world was changing again, yet not enough. The noise vacillated from loud to quiet, between what Jun could and could not accept about the freedom she read on banners under the bridgeway. This village had brought her up; its different roads made the appendages of her body. The village stores, the compartments in her brain. She loved the village because the village had raised her; she had raised the village from fire and ash. The village's redeeming presence was its people, who were always prepared, who never ran amok, who fell ill quietly. They had deemed her vulgar for howling at her husband in public. Her body was emaciated and cold. After years of living in Daejeon, Jun packed her things out of her home and moved north, into an apartment in Seoul, leaving behind her husband and her children.

~

Seoul 1974: Jun, thirty-four, loved to sew in her apartment. She loved to hear the vigorous chants of Christian missionaries on microphones mounted on trucks that burrowed through her streets. Her health surfaced from a tunnel and was flooded by the sun. Her eyes, bright with vitality. She watched people swerve along narrow sidewalks; men and women pulling their shadows in the dance of the city. To all their footsteps, she added her own.

One day, Lee visited to plead with her.

Jun would not open the door. She heard him pacing outside.

He did not go away for hours. He waited before he left. Lee knew that she loved the city, but he could not be with the children by himself. They belonged to her—not him. He was only their father, who could not love them as he used to or wanted to. Lee told her how he felt through the door that divided them. It was her intelligence and her willfulness that he saw in their children. Whenever he thought about her, his chest overflowed with emotions. No other woman would come near their house, their children, or their life together, as it had been when they first married, if she chose to come home. Through the cave of his mouth, there were the glistering eyes of their two sons and two daughters, calling her.

~

Her youngest daughter, my mother, had enrolled in high school in Daejeon, but one school afternoon, she showed up at Jun's door in Seoul.

Jun could tell her daughter had skipped school. She had ridden the two-hour bus alone. Born with Jun's stubborn jaw, her daughter waited outside. Though Jun felt frightened, she was grateful for her daughter's courage.

Her daughter, carrying a basket, dumped it out at her feet. What spilled out were ivory school socks with scissor-cut holes.

Her daughter said, "They're worn down. I don't have socks anymore."

Jun poked her finger through one. "Do they all have such perfect holes?"

"If I don't have socks," her daughter said, "I can't go to school."

Jun counted the socks, seeing her daughter's labor. "How could you be so clever?" Jun muttered.

"I can't go to school," her daughter repeated, "until you fix them—"

"Have somebody else fix them." Jun pushed the basket away.

"There's nobody."

"Do you need money?" Jun asked. "There's a seamstress—"

"No, you have to do it. You have to fix them."

"These are just socks, my daughter."

"You're the best at it, aren't you?"

Jun often boasted about her daughter's wit. "You're too smart to waste away like this."

Through the night, Jun sewed up a dozen pairs of socks and folded them into her daughter's basket. She had to recut many—so hawkish was her daughter with the scissors. Some had been soaked with her daughter's tears. In the morning, Jun nudged her daughter awake and sent her home to Daejeon before the school opened its gates.

The following noon, her daughter knocked again.

As Jun opened the door, her daughter clanged down a heap of bent pots and torn shirts and pants. Instead of going to school, she had banged the pots over the rocks by the house in Daejeon. She had ripped her shirts and slashed through her pants.

Jun asked, "Did your father bring you here?"

"He thinks I'm at school," her daughter said. "But he gave me money."

"What time is the last bus to Daejeon?"

Her daughter stared at the floor as she did when she lied.

"You're betraying your teachers," Jun said sternly. "You'll get on that bus tonight. You're going to school tomorrow."

"Fine. I'll go to school."

"How could you spend your father's money like this?"

Her daughter asked quietly, "When will you come home?"

"Don't sharpen your tongue," Jun replied.

"He said he's sorry," she said. "But you always yell at him and complain."

"This is your father's money. He gives it to you to go to school, to eat your lunch and buy your books," Jun said. "You should be more like your brothers."

Her daughter ignored her. "How could you leave us?" she asked.

"Stop. Don't say anymore," Jun said. "You'll make me cry, and I won't survive it."

She shouted, "You're being selfish!"

"Then go. Get out of here," Jun said. "Take your things."

Her daughter fell to the floor. "No, I'm sorry. I'm sorry—"

"Why can't I be happy?" Jun asked her.

Her daughter cried, but she did not move.

"You're just like your father—greedy. Did you brush your hair? You look dirty, and you stink. How can you be my daughter?" Jun gouged with her words to be certain that her daughter would give up. "One day, you'll have a daughter like you—no—she'll be *worse*," Jun threatened. "Then you'll know that I've come back to spite you."

Jun could not look at her anymore.

Her daughter stood waiting.

"I have to see what I keep inside," Jun said, finally. "Go lie on the couch and sleep."

Jun placed new pots and mended shirts and pants in the center of a large cloth and wrapped it carefully into a bundle for her daughter to carry. On the bus ride back to Daejeon, her daughter would have to set the bundle on the floor, or its weight could bruise her legs. As Jun tied and untied the knot to check the items, she felt her heart might stop at any minute. Her daughter used her strong will, heaved it around every which way, but Jun's feeble heart could not keep up for long. Jun had to scare her daughter away for both their sakes. However, her daughter returned thereafter, missing school for months.

After three months in Seoul, Jun relented and moved back to Daejeon for her daughter who had become sorrowful, sharp-boned. Jun only thought of her children. That winter, the village looked different. It was the snow that caused everything to appear larger than itself. Her footprints left wells, deepened by the moonlight, behind her. Coming to one home, she had abandoned another. Her husband, Lee, welcomed her, waiting before their iron gates. He worked diligently and punctually for her private smile.

~

Two years later, during a heat wave, Jun slowly starved herself.

She caved to a spoonful of porridge from her daughter, who would keep her in Daejeon even when it made her sick. Her daughter's footsteps were uneven throughout the house. Jun heard her pacing outside the bedroom, like her husband. But Jun could not stay long in their home because she could hardly get out of bed. As her daughter matriculated into the next year of high school, Jun was hospitalized for high blood pressure.

Her daughter ditched her classes to visit Jun in the hospital. She asked Jun to be reasonable, more forgiving toward her father. Her daughter's hand cooled her cheek. She said that Jun might feel better if she let go of her hurt and her long-held resentment. Jun spotted a troublesome wrinkle on her daughter's forehead. That wrinkle bore daughters, who gave more wrinkles by fighting; those with smooth foreheads bore sons, who compounded smoothness by restriction. In the end, there was no escaping a mother's face.

Though Lee disapproved of his daughter's interest in the city, and hoped she would marry decidedly soon and busy herself with children of her own, Jun longed for the day she could point out her striking daughter on television.

In the hospital, Jun stopped chewing her food or summoning the effort. When her daughter looked away, Jun spit out the mush. When Jun did eat something, her stomach brought it up. Jun only wished she had never scolded her daughter for coming to her.

Though sudden fog obscured her view, Jun instructed her daughter to finish high school and college, if nothing else. Her daughter begged her to be lighter, emptier. She believed these adjustments could save Jun's life. They could return home, where everyone waited. What Jun did not say was how she wanted her daughter to be anybody but Jun.

Daejeon 1980: Jun died of heartbreak in her hospital bed at the age of forty.

~

Back then, the villagers did not call it an aneurysm.

In the village, they gossiped: heartbreak this and that. Heartbreak made ghosts. Villagers scurried into their houses on quick-moving feet and bowed their heads deeper when greeting strangers, should the stranger be a reincarnation of Jun, or should Jun herself wander their roads, creeks, bus routes, and schoolyards; hair salons, grocery stores, and temples. The air was like a runny nose, cicadas crying.

Both religious practitioners and non-churchgoers burned a candle on their windowsill and another candle across the dirt path to ward off her spirit as forcefully as it could go. They fanned the smoke, purifying the space. The whole town lit up with fear. But the more they did, the less it mattered. Though they were reminded of that ostentatious woman's ghost, it bewildered the village to continue. Where was the poor woman? Her stilettos and her tearful singing voice? To make her disappear, they must wait.

As months passed, the villagers tossed away the candles in their jars. Words about the woman, they ignored or flung outside. The villagers prayed fastidiously, but less so in the winter. They bundled up, slept long hours. The worst was when they called it heartbreak. It forced an ending to a story meant to pass over the village like a cold, like something to be forgotten.

~

In October 1983, three years after Jun's death, Lee was driving home from a fishing trip late one night. It was windy, raining, and his car slipped off the roadway. It tipped past the cliff and tumbled down into the creek below. The villagers fished out his bloated body floating down the water. Nobody witnessed the accident. There was no investigation. Maybe a guilt-ridden, drunken night, or he had been en route to his lover's bosom, until a semi hurtled into his lane to make him swerve.

Perhaps Lee had recognized his wife in his rearview mirror. In its reflection, Jun mouthed the words to a song, twirling barefoot over the wet asphalt behind him. Lee remembered she loved to dance in her nightgown on rainy nights. When water filled the wrecked car, perhaps Lee did not reach for the door. He stayed where he was, his suit lifting off his body underwater. His tie swam by his chin as he gazed into the mirror until Jun sang her final note. To Lee, the song was about her loving him, about how she knew that he loved her; she knew everything there was to know about love, and she was sorry it was all true.

Meanwhile, his daughter was sitting alone at an outdoor bar near her college dormitory. She woke up in her room, aided by tea from her sister's hand, surrounded by her thin, clear-voiced brothers, who coaxed her to another room, where waiting for her was a black-ribboned photograph of her father beside the one of her mother.

~

Daejeon 2016, thirty-three years later: my mother returned to that place to exhume the bodies of her mother and father from their burial sites. Her sister and brothers had been phoning her in the States. They dreamed that Lee called out to them while cold and shivering violently. They asked for my mother's help in moving the bodies.

When the site operator uncovered Lee's body from the hill where he lay buried, the operator discovered that his frail bones had been steeped in water for the past year.

"The river," my mother said, "was running through his body." She began to cry. "Isn't there enough justice in death? Why this river, freezing his corpse?" My mother squeezed her eyes shut. "How can it go through the site of his remains?"

Lee's bones were black, withered.

However, beside him, a foot away, was Jun's body.

The river turned into a stream and veered away. It refused to touch her.

Jun had kept her bones beautifully preserved. They were soft brown like sweet-smelling dirt, and her wrappings were still intact to keep her warm. She lay with her hands neatly crossed, poised. She appeared at attention, but comfortably, as if she had all the time in the world to observe. Her head was slightly cocked, as if she were smiling inside, as if there were a needle in her mouth. She looked elegant, well rested. Even the operator felt so moved to describe the sight before him. He had never seen, in his long years, such serene earth. He would never forget her. For Lee's military service, the country offered Jun and Lee a public reburial at the treasured Daejeon National Cemetery, not in haste as before but with loving, tempered regret, the highest prestige.

7

Hello?

Pure white snow fell overnight (*during the night*). All the world is white. Your dad has to leave for work, but I'm worried about his car. They have to clear the snow, you see. There are 15 centimeters of snow piled onto the hood of the car. Here? It's morning. After your dad leaves for work, Mommy will drive to the countryside. I'm meeting Auntie and my *cousins*. I told you, right? I'll have to take an *absence* for Japanese class tomorrow. That's worrisome, too. There are 4 students in class (*including me*), but 2 students had something come up (*excuse*) so they said they can't come to class anymore. Then, the *class* might be discontinued. I've been trying to study a subject, but now this. Upsetting, isn't it? Even so, I'm going to learn. Because there are other classes, too.

What're you up to *lately*? You finished your *finals*. You had a dance *performance*. And you're getting along with your friends? Tell me if you need anything when Mommy visits. Ah, I said I'd write down some Japanese for you, but I didn't, didn't I? *Right here*!

("Nani ga hoshii desu ka." What do you want to have?)

("Nani ga shitai desu ka." What do you want to do?)

("Okane ga hoshii desu." I want to have money.)

("Sekai ryokou ((world travel)) ga shitai desu." I want to travel the world.)

How about it? Easy, isn't it? As you go, it gets harder but it's fun for now.

For the next letter, I'll write it after I get back from the countryside. Since I'm going for (2 *nights and* 3 *days*) (7th, 8th, and 9th), I'll write on Friday.

Just now I got a call, they can't go to the countryside. It's snowing so much the roads are blocked, and they can't get through. It's too much. Isn't it? Our country's back roads are narrow and cemented. Can't do anything about it, I guess. I'll have to get in touch with Auntie and my cousins in a bit to figure out what to do.

Little Uncle said he's moving tomorrow. I couldn't help him. I feel very sorry and I'm worried. *This year*, I'd like for Little Uncle to live comfortably. Big Uncle's doing well now.

They called again, we're gathering at my cousin's house in Icheon. But there's still a big problem. I don't know if the car will budge or not. Your Auntie from Daejeon already boarded the bus. Aigo. It's hard to meet my family.

Anyway, I've got to run. On a day the world is white, I'll have to ask for some *luck*. "Please look after my babies' health, especially let my Eun Ji get along well. Let Eun Ji get accepted into the *college* she specifically wants." Ah! There's more. "Thank you. Thank you for everything." Mommy will have fun and as soon as I come back, I'll write another letter. *Be happy*!

Mom
February 7, 2006

Hello ?

밤새 (during the night) 하얀눈이 많이 왔구나.

온세상이 하얗다.

아빠 출근(出勤)해야 하는데 차 땜에 걱정이다.

눈 다 치워야 하잖아.

차 위에도 눈이 15cm 정도 쌓였거든.

지금? 아침이야.

아빠 출근하고 나면 엄마는 시골에 간다.

이모하고 cousin들 만나러 가거든. 얘기 했지?

할 수 없이 내일 일본어 학원은 absence 이다.

그것도 걱정이야.

학원에 4명 있거든, (including me)

근데 2명이 사정(excuse)이 생겨서 이제부터 못나온대.

그러면 class가 없어질 수도 있어

모처럼 뭔가 배우려고 하는데 많아

속상 하겠지?

그래도 배울거야. 다는데도 있으니까.

너는 lately 뭐하고 지내?

final 도 끝났고. performance도 했고,

친구들 하고는 잘 지내구?

엄마 갈때 뭐 필요한것 있으면 말해.

참, 일본말 적어 준다고 하고선 안해줬지 ?

right here !

(" 나니가 호시이데스까." 무엇을 갖고 싶습니까?)

(" 나니가 시따이데스까." 무엇을 하고 싶습니까?)

(" 오까네가 호시이데스 " 돈이 갖고 싶습니다.)

(" 세까이료꼬우 (세계여행) 가 시따이데스 ")

　　　　　　　세계여행이 하고 싶습니다.

How about it? 쉽지?
갈수록 어려워 지지만 아직 재미있어.
다음 편지는 시골에 갔다와서 쓸께.
2박 3일 (2nights and 3days) 가니까 (7.8.9)
금요일에 쓸께. ——
금방 전화 왔는데 시골에 못간대.
눈이 너무 많이 타서 길이 막혀서 못간대.
너무하다. 2지?
우리나라 시골길은 작고 시멘트길 이잖아.
할 수 없지 뭐.
좀 있다가 언니들 하고 연락해서 어떻게 해야지.
작은 삼촌은 내일 이사 한대.
도와주지 못했어. 많이 미안하고 걱정도 돼.
this year 에는 삼촌이 좀 잘살았으면 좋겠다.
큰 삼촌네는 이제 괜찮은데 말야.
또 전화 왔는데 이천 언니집으로 모인대.
그래도 큰일이다. 차가 움직일래나 모르겠다.
대전 이모는 벌써 버스 탔대.
에이고, 언니들 만나기 힘들다.
Anyway 나가봐야지. 온세상이 하얀날 luck을
빌어야 겠다.
'우리 새끼를 건강하게 보살펴 주시고 특히 우리은지가
잘 지낼 수 있게 해주십시e, 특별히 은지가
원하는 College 에도 합격 하게 해주십시e'
아! 또 있다
'감사 합니다. 뭐든지 감사 합니다'
엄마 잘 지내고 와서 바로 다시 편지 할께.
be happy!

mom
2006. 2. 7. 9AM

8

After visiting my mother, I arrived in Japan later that month at Narita Airport. I was seventeen when I decided to enroll in a summer program at an international school to learn Japanese. An elderly woman with fierce eyes, wearing khakis and a visor, showed me a map of Tokyo where she had marked two circles, east and west of each other, one for my hotel in Okachimachi, the other for my school in Shinanomachi. On the flight from Incheon to Narita, I had gotten sick in the cabin, unable to digest the bento meal. The crew apologized, but they could not give me medicine on board. For two hours, my head was bent over the lavatory toilet while hanging on the handrail during turbulence. Outside the plane window, white tail winds whipped against dark-bright rain.

I had a Japanese pocket dictionary, a bag of clothes, and nothing else. The woman rubbed my cold hands with hers and said I would not see her again unless something terrible happened to me. The bus I rode plunged through the night roads. Squeezed into back rows with tightly knit sleeping passengers, the strange woman's words accompanied me. One row opened after the Nihonbashi stop. I lay across it and slept beside the others.

~

I was strict about my Japanese. Before dawn, I left my hotel room in Okachimachi, careful not to wake my roommate, but sleep was scant on five-foot-long beds where I lay diagonally on my left or right side, switching every other day. Near the train station, an indoor mall opened its shuttered gates. Through the gates, I entered an empty coffee shop with a canopy of hanging vines. On a high stool at the coffee bar, I memorized ten pages of my Japanese dictionary, copying down two hundred words. There were six thousand words all together, divided into categories: eating, driving, home, and others. After three hours, I smoked a cigarette as I walked on the uphill road to the train station and headed toward Shinanomachi. When school let out, I returned to the coffee shop to go over my pages in the evening. How close the words sounded to my ear as I spoke them. I would learn the language the way one might learn a person. My first word, an apology, taught me how to stop strangers so I could ask for help.

For eight days, I refused to dine at a restaurant until I could order properly. If I could not learn a language, why bother with a complete meal? I stuck to this rule even when on the verge of storming an udon bar at which salarymen and students ate in silence. I watched a boy no bigger than me, at a ramen stand outside my hotel, scarf down a tremendous pile of noodles and, in five minutes, return his empty bowl to the counter and disappear beyond the linen curtain door. On my hotel rooftop, I paced in my *yukata*, having water and rice balls from the convenience store. I did not throw up anything; I refused to eat if needed because I thought it mature to withhold rather than waste, to choose rather than give up. After a smoke, I set myself to the task of ordering for the first time: I must pronounce the words comfortably, say them formally but friendly, in a tone of polite asking, seeking reassurance, apologetic yet eager to be heard.

At a hideaway outside the Okachimachi station, after ten days had passed, I sat myself alone at a bar top on a night clamoring with salarymen. Above the din of hollow glasses clinking, I ordered a shoyu ramen from the chef across from me in Japanese. I ignored his eyes and fixed my gaze on the bowl he set on the bar. I expected our exchange to end until I asked for the bill. But the chef asked me whether I had taken breakfast that morning, or any meals—a conversation I had not learned in my book. I replied in Japanese my desire to immerse myself in studies, using an open hand gesture in front. My elbows or

arms did not take up space and I kept my posture straight to
show that I was listening. There were words, choices I made:
isshokenmei for persistence, not aggression; hesitation to de-
note intelligence; for deference, speaking with hands rather
than eyes. The chef pointed to his nose, indicating himself,
and said he understood me perfectly. He praised my forbear-
ance and restraint. An employee, stirring noodles, corrected
a word I had used. *Chotto*, a little. "The word isn't literal,"
he said in Japanese. "Closer to 'kind of' or 'that's a bit . . .' to
deny a request or consider a reply." He told me *chotto* gives
away foreigners because of its mistranslation. The chef added,
"*Chotto* isn't a measure but an apology."

They heard me despite my mistakes and offered words. I
studied their hand gestures—how they chopped their hand
and waved it back and forth to say "no." The next day, before
I touched the bar, the chef served me a shoyu ramen. "What
new words do you have today?" he asked. Three weeks passed
like this. The barista asked after my studies, overfilled my cup.
The owner at a bag shop noticed me eyeing a duffel and gifted
it at hardly any cost. They called out to me, "Koh-san," waving whenever I crossed the road toward the Okachimachi station, as if I were a daughter of the neighborhood. My Japanese
grew into a spectacular tree. My tone bowed with my body:
Sou, sou, sou. I gestured with integrity so that my hands never
pointed to anyone but myself. Outside of Shinanomachi, I
was on my own in coffee shops, markets, parks, temples, and
I was learning—slowly, but still learning—and I had never
before felt that I was not so alone.

~

Six blocks from my hotel, outside the Okachimachi station, an outdoor fashion plaza had stages for rock shows, bargain stores, and zigzag escalators that churned like rows of teeth. The center of the plaza was packed with *takoyaki* and meat bun stands where workers shouted, their voices cleaving the grounds. The floor of the plaza had been painted green. Everyone, as if taking part in a Noh play, took their proper place. They walked from one store to the next. A finger pointed to the air, followed by laughter. Foreigners came and went, but the chef and barista and shopkeeper looked at them differently. The chef and the others disguised themselves from foreigners with a cheerfulness and decorum that drew a thick line between strangers—such as the sound of a plate set on one's table when one does not know whose hand guided it there safely.

With me, they talked through the night. They sat next to me, watered me with conversation. You cannot cook a grain of rice by itself. It was from them that I learned the word *umareru*, to be born. I told them that I was born in America. The shopkeeper confessed that despite my country of origin, she noticed my sternness and appreciated my isolation. But my schoolteacher in Shinanomachi said, "The workers are confused. They wonder if you're truly American or Korean. To them," my teacher explained, "from your single-mindedness and your downward eyes and the rising tip of your nose, you are Japanese. Look at your thick hair, how you *dread* pleasure for the sake of pleasure." My teacher was certain of this even though I myself could not verify it. Otherwise, the workers would not have paid me any attention, she told me. If I had protested, they might have asked me, "Why did you come to Japan if you didn't want to be Japanese?" But they were careful not to say a word—to let me stave off a bit longer the question of who I was.

~

I was my mother's daughter. The same face except for subtle differences one would notice on close study. Though her lips were fuller, my eyes were wider. Her brows framed her face gently while mine bordered my face like a box. I shaved the arches of my eyebrows to soften them like hers. I looked like my mother, my mother like her mother, but no one would say I looked like my mother's mother. My mother drank heavily after her mother's death. My father, her friend then, dragged her out of bars regularly. But one night, a man tossed a remark at her. Right there, my father brawled with him and nearly died when the man broke a beer bottle and stabbed my father in the throat, barely missing the jugular. The man had two friends with him. Both joined in the beating of my father. My mother called her brothers to rescue him. After that day, they got married. I was my father's daughter because there was in me, other than my face, this love for my mother.

~

After one month in Tokyo, I was strolling through Ueno Park on a date. I was seventeen and Touma, a scuba diving instructor, was thirty-three. Touma worked as a tour guide at the school where I was taking classes and preparing to give a speech in Japanese about my time in Tokyo. Touma was six foot, wore glasses, a messenger bag, and strode beside me in brown sandals. I pictured his already tall frame in long snorkeling fins swimming in the sea as we shopped for shoes together.

We had passed each other in the office or the hallway a dozen times without a word between us. One day, the girls at school squirmed to see him waiting outside our classroom. He reprimanded me in front of the girls, who watched us from inside the classroom, giddy with envy. Touma urged me to get another pair of shoes since my feet were reduced to shambles from roaming around in open-toed slippers.

Instead of shoes, I picked up a first aid kit in a souvenir shop across the park. We got beer and sushi at an old-style bar before he pointed to the famous Ueno Zoo nearby. The flash of his muscled arm beneath his shirt embarrassed me.

Next to Ueno Zoo, we hung wishes at the temple. I do not recall telling Touma a single thing about myself. We went back and forth sharing impressions of the things around us. The wind tossed the wooden plaques inscribed with wishes he read aloud. It was urgent to him that I grasp the significance of where I stood now. When we looked at each other, his eyes leapt about my face, avoiding me. Only when I turned away did I catch him glimpsing at me directly. In my periphery, he became daring. He walked closer, then stepped back as soon as I faced him to speak. It did not mean Touma was nervous. I understood this. Rather, he was polite. He said without speaking that his reservations made him somebody to trust. It encouraged me to imagine lying together. When he noticed me staring, I apologized, and my apology must have meant a similar thing to him because he blushed.

Despite my attention to him, and his quiet flirtation with me, I was not with Touma at all. I was strolling with my grandmother, my father's mother, on this same road she had described to me as the place of her childhood. While my parents had worked in Milpitas, my grandmother rocked me on her lap and whispered that she would like to go back one day to that town and that zoo where she had grown up as a Japanese girl.

"When you leave, will you visit me?" Touma faced the entrance of the zoo, where the sign read *Closed*. He pointed out the large lilies in the pond across the street. Touma was Korean and employed by the school, but he did not hang around the Korean students or speak Korean freely. He asked me in Japanese, "Or will you forget me entirely?"

When I laughed, he put two fingers on his chest, and said the word for grandfather, *ojiisan*. "Do you think I'm an old man?" he asked me.

I nodded and replied with the same word in Korean, *harabuji*, then added in Japanese, "Are you afraid you'll never see me again?"

"You tease me so much," he said. "Your Japanese must be getting better if you can make fun of me. You feel comfortable here, don't you?"

As we walked, he stopped and looked down at my feet.

"You're bleeding," he scolded. "Can't you buy a pair of shoes?"

"If no one sees my feet up close, it doesn't matter."

"What if you need it?" It was inconceivable to him that I would not buy what I needed. "You're making other people worry about you. Shouldn't you be more considerate?"

"Why would I need it?" I asked. "I don't need anything."

"You *need* shoes. Walking shoes."

"You're embarrassing me—"

"Because it's unreasonable, don't you think? I thought you were different. I can't understand—you're being stubborn, like a typical Korean. Especially when it's right there, they sell shoes on the road. We passed a *dozen* stands."

"I can still wear these. What's wrong with the ones I have?"

"They're hurting you," he insisted. "Throw them away—"

"No." I walked ahead of him.

Touma caught up to me. "What will you do when your feet fall off?" He demanded to know. "When you're driving a car and the wheels go?"

I headed in the direction of the station. I remembered that I had not memorized my pages today. My dictionary waited for me at the hotel in Okachimachi.

~

One night in Davis, my brother and I, twenty and sixteen, had been fighting in the car again. It was on a long stretch of the highway toward the house. My brother turned off the radio to hear me better. He asked me to say it again.

"I hate you."

My brother's head clicked like an abacus, slinging his thoughts into place before he lowered the window. "You want to know why you're here?" he asked me. "Because they wanted a better life—"

My brother gassed the car. My hand flew to the door handle.

He asked, "Do you think they'd care if we died?" Speeding, his speech slowed. "I'm tired, too." He was driving toward whatever he saw in his mind, and I was only a passenger. "You tell me if you want to live or not."

Maybe he asked so I would stop him from causing a wreck. But I never stopped anybody from doing anything.

My brother and I made it back to the house. We arrived in silence and intact—not because we wanted to live—but because I had not given him an answer. I opened the windows to air out the rooms. He plugged in the vacuum, lifted the furniture, and moved the chairs out of his path. He left behind neat, parallel lines across the carpet. Cleaning was not a chore but an act of atonement. In the morning, we hauled ourselves into his car and he drove me to school.

~

Touma still came with me to my stop at the Okachimachi station.

"Maybe it's the other way around," Touma said. "I'm the one you don't need."

"I want to see you again." I knew he cared for me.

Touma smiled. "Promise me you'll practice," he said. "If you lose your Japanese, then you'll forget all about me and this place. With your tongue goes your memory."

I accused him of being married, and the joke made him laugh.

"Don't pretend you're jealous," he warned. "Or you'll make my heart flutter."

Touma waved goodbye. His elbow was anchored in the air, his forearm swinging back and forth, but his fingers held no space between them. His hand was stiff. He waved a blank page, and I knew it was gestures like this one that meant nothing.

~

My last week in Tokyo, the school organized a trip to a *ryokan* away from the city.

Some eighty of us were separated by gender before entering the outdoor *onsen*, divided by rows of bamboo trees. We entered naked save for the towels we wrapped around our hair, tucking away the loose strands. There was an indoor bath, overflowing with springwater. A window gave a view of a waterfall a short distance from the bath. I was staring out when a frog leapt down from someplace onto a rock beside me. Then the frog disappeared toward the forest. I thought about the speech I would give at the school, but I still felt that I had missed something. We rejoined the others in a large private room with tatami mats and floor tables. Our heads bowed over our yukatas. Our cheeks glowed.

At the table where I sat with four boys and three girls, we spoke only in Japanese. We complimented the tableware and kaiseki courses set before us by a dozen staff waiting at the ends of the room. Eighty little stone grills with plates of thinly sliced short rib arrived from the kitchen, filling the hallways and every adjoining room with the scent of sweet soy marinade. After a shot of sake, the boys and girls began talking to each other in Korean. They were older students, late twenties to midthirties. They had met at the school and become friends learning Japanese. One girl laughed, saying it was better to study here than to be pressured to marry at home. One boy said he came for the better job market in Japan for hairstylists. They all stood up when I responded in Korean. "Koh-san, I thought it was short for *kodomo*, like a child. But of course, Koh is a Korean last name!" the boy said and clapped loudly. "You're so cozy with the teachers, but you're one of us." They wanted to show me something. They said we were a special group of people who had come together. They said we had found each other, and I had begun to feel that it was true.

We retreated into a reserved room inside the ryokan that was spacious, a dozen tatami mats long, with a low ceiling and floor lights. The center of the room was on a raised platform. There was an ikebana plant in the corner. We flailed our arms in the air to impersonate the plant, our eyes became flora and our legs were stalks, before we collapsed again as ourselves. We drank Japanese sake, Korean soju, and Chinese *baijiu*. The baijiu won the test of strength as neither artful nor uplifting, only hard and undeniable. Laughing, we did not cover our mouths, burning with the kerosene taste of esters. Their names came one after another: Jae Woo, Kang Min, Moon Sik, Byung Ho, and the girls, Yoon Hee, Se Jin, and Min Jung. To put me in order, they asked for my age and birthday.

"Baijiu can solve anything," Byung Ho, the smallest one, said in Korean as he sipped his glass slowly. "It's the key to diplomacy around the world. Don't you think so?"

Min Jung poured us water. "You get a few Koreans in a room and we're already talking about diplomacy?" she asked. "I guess the obvious thing is that we have to be grateful. We're Koreans in Japan—drinking and laughing in a ryokan."

"Don't be such a downer," Byung Ho said. "You sound like my parents—and my grandparents. The past is a long time ago. Have you heard a Japanese person say they hate us during this whole trip? Kaneda-san and the teachers are too busy worrying that we hate *them*. My Japanese friend in Akihabara said the same thing to me the other day."

Jae Woo laughed. "Don't worry about him, Min Jung. Byung Ho's just saying that because Japanese girls love Korean boys. He's never gotten so much attention before."

Byung Ho gestured wildly. "It's not my fault I want to stay here. They think I look like a lead in a Korean drama. They like that I can't be loyal, and I can't fall in love!"

Jae Woo struck Byung Ho's head and Byung Ho dramatically toppled backward and off the platform, making us laugh. A moment later, he returned and refilled his glass.

I struck a match and lit a cigarette from a pack I had gotten at a vending machine outside the ryokan. We shared an ashtray on the table.

They asked me to say something in English. They already knew English from classes they had taken in Korea, but I began a conversation: "Hi, how are you? How do you like it here in Japan?"

Jae Woo replied in English, using Byung Ho's higher pitched voice: "Korean girls don't like me. They don't want to marry me. Do you have any advice?"

"I don't like him," Min Jung said in English, and pointed at them. "I don't like both. I like a Korean man who is a gentleman, like James Bond."

"Good." Yoon Hee, the eldest, gave a thumbs-up.

We used our gestures, but we were amazed, if not at speaking in English with other Koreans, then that we were doing these things in Japan. Could we feel so delighted if we had met any other way? The ashes collected and I smiled even if I knew they would appear this one time in my life.

Like the others, they would go, their faces made strange again. Solitude was an aspect of my life, though it seemed I could forget it with laughter.

Yoon Hee switched to Korean and said to me, "Ah, if I were seventeen, I'd go all over the world like you. Maybe I could've written a book about my travels."

"You can't put the old with the young in a room," Byung Ho said.

Min Jung said to Byung Ho, "You worry about your height!"

"I'm not jealous," Yoon Hee defended herself. "I just don't want to get married. Your husband's a stranger. Your children are baggage. Your house is a mess."

Min Jung said, "Nothing's worse than being my mother's daughter."

Se Jin poured Min Jung another drink. Yoon Hee slouched at the table.

"You should hear how she sends my little brother to high school. 'If it rains, I'll pick you up in my car. Don't push yourself or you'll get sick,'" Min Jung parroted, and then downed her drink. She dusted off droplets of soju that got on her shirt. "When she sees me, all she complains about is how all the other mothers brag about their daughter's husbands. When, for heaven's sake, will I ever give her something to brag about?"

Byung Ho, taking the blame, pointed to himself. "I know I'm a piece of shit. But even my mother wouldn't say you're good enough for me!" He fanned himself. "That's how it's always been, hasn't it? Cheer up, Min Jung. Wait until your mother grows old. You'll see who she needs then. Her son, infatuated with his young wife, or her neglected single daughter. Let her see who will take her in."

Min Jung grimaced. "I hope she realizes it soon. For her sake."

Yoon Hee pointed her pinky at me. "Don't Americans send their parents to an old people's home?" She collapsed back onto the floor. "What an idea!"

Jae Woo got down on one knee and proposed to me. "Maybe you will marry *me*?" he asked me in Korean. He said that if I did not get engaged now, then I might become like Yoon Hee, or embittered like Min Jung. Days later, Jae Woo would propose to me again. He would cut his hair and take me to his favorite Italian restaurant in Akihabara. But now, his bandana unraveled from his forehead and fell around his collar. His long tresses touched his shoulders, and his eyes, narrow and shiny, dared me to doubt him. The others stopped laughing. Jae Woo said he was already thirty and that we could go to Paris, where he would open a hair salon, and we could live together while wandering freely and imaginatively. If I chose to return to America, then I would think about him and our possible life, only to be filled with regret.

To get more cigarettes, I swam out of the room and into the hallway toward the elevators. Byung Ho quipped about my shot glass, perfectly full and left behind. It was innocently that he chased after me in the hall, midway to a jog on his skinny legs. He would not let anyone get away from a drink, and it was likely that somebody else in the room had encouraged him. One must be sensitive to drinking etiquette with elders.

In the hall, Byung Ho grabbed my hand to drag me back to that same room. I understood that he was only playing. His humor was obvious to me as he seized my wrist. And he did not yank on it, or never meant to if he did. He pulled as a gesture of harmless drunken banter and nothing more.

But the scuba diving instructor, Touma, saw something else when he stepped out of the elevator onto the floor just as Byung Ho lunged for me. Touma, stiff-jawed with balled fists, appeared enraged. There was no appropriate context for Byung Ho to steal my hand, shouting in another language, in a ryokan no less. Touma's face had the look of recognition as he stared at Byung Ho, who was unaware of the damage. To Byung Ho, Touma was a Japanese instructor. When Touma yanked my other arm and jerked me away from him, Byung Ho seemed bewildered—why had this Japanese instructor lost his decorum? Touma, for his part, was too furious to hear me giving him answers.

Byung Ho did not realize that Touma knew me and that we were acquainted. He watched the Japanese instructor grab my arm and then barked at Touma, pushed him backward. When Byung Ho reached for me again, this time to get me away from Touma, it was Touma who shoved him against the wall. Byung Ho flushed red, and Touma's face appeared as if it would never come out of its grimace.

Earlier, a drinking party, a peaceful night. But Touma and Byung Ho shouted at each other in Japanese. Four other instructors arrived and held Byung Ho and Touma apart. Byung Ho then said something in Korean, not knowing that Touma could understand his words, but his words must have been cruel.

Yoon Hee, Se Jin, and Min Jung dashed out into the hall, urging me to get to safety. They gathered me into the elevator. They pushed the button, any button. They wanted to get away. "Hurry. Go. Go!" Eyes wide and white, they were terrified. They had only heard the two men shouting, then panicked that the police would come. The elevator doors would not close. Jae Woo, Kang Min, and Moon Sik came out into the hall, wrenching Byung Ho free from Touma's grasp. The girls were frantic, tugging on me.

Suddenly, there was a crash as Touma's arm—the one he had waved gently at the end of our date—swung widely into Byung Ho's jaw, followed by a disgusting pop, and the others wailed, leaning on each other like houses worn by the weather, then rising again, arms going up, reaching overhead, seeking freedom from the mass of limbs, all snatching fiercely at each other. I had not been truly frightened until I heard the crack of bone, saw the sharp twist of Byung Ho's neck, and heard the screams that erupted from the narrow hall, before the elevator doors closed and all the sounds and sights closed with it.

The girls huddled around me in disbelief, then solemnity. "We're not out of danger," Yoon Hee said, and called Kang Min as we got off on another floor. He had caught Byung Ho as he collapsed. There was yelling on the other end of the line. Then Kang Min hung up. Se Jin ushered us to her own room down the hall.

This room was the same as the other one. Yoon Hee tried calling again but there was no answer. In a given situation, we might have responded differently. But in Japan, we could only wait for news. Min Jung, who had been quiet, asked whether the police were outside. She wondered if there was an ambulance. "Won't they have questions for us? What if they take us into custody? If we go to prison in this country, then who will get us out?" Min Jung shook her head. "The police have different rules. This place is dangerous for people like us. They have another language for people like you and me."

Se Jin poured water for each of us. Yoon Hee tried calling another time while Min Jung shouted. "Stop soothing each other," she said. "We're in a lot of trouble. Do you know what they used to do to girls like us? Who'd care if they killed us now, we're not even in our own country." I thought of the outdoor mall, where the shopkeeper, chef, and barista must be closing their doors now. The woman with the visor must be searching for me.

Yoon Hee put the phone on the table. Se Jin cried while Min Jung recounted the sound of that snapping jaw. "He's not dead, is he? Probably not, but even so, they're going to blame us, won't they? To be Korean here of all places. *Ha*, to be women, trapped!"

Looking around, Min Jung changed her mind. "Stop crying already," she said to Se Jin. "We're just imagining things. Everything will be cleared up in the morning."

Se Jin was the only one to drink the water she had poured. The phone rang and Yoon Hee learned that Byung Ho and the instructor were taken back to the city. They would be sorted out by the school. The silence only lasted a minute. Se Jin, who had been quiet, ruffled her hair and looked me right in the eyes. "Tell us what happened," she said to me, lowering her voice. "You were there in the hallway when everything started." The others stared at me with suspicion. Min Jung blocked the door, arms crossed. And Se Jin recalled that the instructor, who assaulted one of their friends, that lunatic instructor, an obvious traitor, who shouted profanities in Korean and Japanese, called my name over and over again.

~

On my last day, I gave my speech at the school in Japanese.

I remember describing the subway. When the doors opened, the attendants on the platform shoved us inside. Squashed together, all of us strangers, we traveled to our stops. No one dared to move into a better spot or empty out until the doors opened. Then it became practice. The doors opened and closed. During the night, in my dreams, they opened and closed. One must not resist being forced together just as one must not hesitate when parting. My schoolteacher waited for me outside. "What you say is true, but who will talk to you in Japanese again? Won't you feel so alone?" she sobbed. "Your fate is to become a hunter—you will look for it everywhere, anywhere you go. Your hunger will teach you what you've lost."

9

My beloved daughter, look here.

Hi?

Your dad's funny, isn't he? When Mommy says, "Isn't our daughter too pretty?" he goes, "Well, she is pretty to you because she's yours." Then, after visiting you, he became deeply concerned all of a sudden. "Our Eun Ji is getting too pretty, isn't she?" Mommy is worried, too. Prettiness is God's *"gift"* to you, but mindfulness, honesty, skillfulness, and good-heartedness are earned by your own (*efforts*). The more you're given, the more you must carry *modesty* and remain *humble*. You know what Mommy's telling you, right? Yes, I'm saying don't put up your good looks for others but pile up your talents.

What a relief they say babies growing up in America do not brag. Mommy lived in Korea for a long time, and thoughts like that come to mind. In a crowded country, people are busy competing (*competition*), pushing past each other here and there, it's maddening. It's become a society where I have to assert and promote myself (*propaganda*) to be recognized. People living in America are a little easier going. Because it's a bigger country? Each and every person works diligently on their own while living quietly. Right? Korea has its good sides, too. The people here take an interest in one another and practice great loyalty and warm affection. Family. Friends. Neighbors. Everyone sticks close together, you know.

During the big holidays (New Years, Thanksgiving, Christmas), Mommy and your Dad are lonely, too. Because Eun Ji and Chang Hyun are not here. You guys miss us too, right? At least my babies have grown up successfully for me, and I feel delighted and happy, but once in a while, no, very often, I desperately want to see you guys. Now, there's one month left? While waiting for that day, I'll have to live harder.

Your brother has grown up, too. Working for a company will give him good experiences. To be honest, Chang Hyun is already an adult now. My Eun Ji is still a baby! (Hu hu, isn't it a tease?) Don't get ticked off and look at this picture!

They say her name is Baby Lamb Lisa.

The name's like my Catholic name, but doesn't she look like you? I just copied the drawing. Don't embarrass me.

You say you're practicing your songs? I heard singing a lot is good for your *lungs*. You live healthier and longer. When Mommy goes to America, let's sing lots. Tomorrow, I'll go find out about a karaoke *CD*. I'd like to get one for sure, but if I can't, when I move back to America next year, I will buy a brand-new karaoke machine for you and bring it with me. Whenever Eun Ji comes home, she can sing. Be well, and see you in the next letter. Bye.

Mom
January 31, 2006

사랑하는 내딸 보아라.

안녕?

아빠 옳기지?

엄마가 "우리딸 너무예쁘지?" 그러면 아빠가

"당신 딸이라 그렇지 뭐" 이랬었거든.

그런데 이번에 보고 있다더니 너무 너무 걱정되신거야.

우리 윤지 정말 너무 예뻐지는거 아냐?

엄마도 걱정이다.

예쁜건 하느님이 주신 'gift' 이고

온바르고 성실하고 능력있고 좋은사람이 되는건

자기 노력 (effort) 인데 그럴수록 modesty (겸손)하고

humble 해야 되거든.

엄마가 무슨 말 하는지 알지?

그래, 예쁜거 내세우지 말고 실력을 쌓으란 얘기지.

다행히. 미국에서 큰 애들은 잔난척을 안한다는 거지.

엄마가 한국에 오래 산다보니. 그런 생각이 든다.

좋은땅에서 자기들끼리 경쟁 (competition) 하느라

이리 치고 저리치고 난리잖아.

나를 내세우고 자기 피알 (propaganda)을

해야만 알아주는 사회가 됐거든.

미국에 사는 사람들이 그런더 너그러운것 같애.

땅이 커서 그런가?

모두 모두 조용히 자기 할일을 하면서 열심히

살아가고 있잖아. 그치?

한국도 좋은 점은 있어.

모두에게 서로 관심 갖어 주고, 정도 많고,

가족. 친구. 이웃 모두 가깝게 지내잖아.

이런 큰 명절 (새해. 추억. 크리스마스 등) 에는
엄마 아빠도 힘들다.
은지하고 창현이가 없어서.
너희들도 그렇지?
다행이 내 새끼들이 훌륭하게 자라 주어서
더욱 기쁘고 행복하지만 가끔은 아니, 아주 자주
너희들이 너무 보고싶구나.
이제 한 달 남았지?
그날을 기다리며 열심히 살아야지.
아빠도 기특하다.
회사에 다니면 좋은 경험이 될거야.
사실 창현이는 이제 어른이잖아.
우리 은지는 아직 애기! (후후 악오르지?)

이 그림 보고 삐지지마!
얘 이름이 '아기 양 리나' 래.
이름은 엄마랑 같은데 은지 닮았지?
그냥 보고 그린거야.
흉보면 안돼.
노래 연습 많이 한다구?
노래는 많이 부르면 lungs 에도 좋대.
건강하게 오래 살구.
엄마 미국에 가면 노래도 많이 부르자.
내일은 나가서 노래방 C.D 알아볼께.
꼭 구했으면 좋겠는데, 만약 못구하면
내년에 미국에 돌아갈때 새 가라오께 기계
사가지고 가야겠다. 은지가 집에 올때마다
노래 부를수 있게 말야.
잘 지내고 다음 편지에서 또 만나자. 안녕.

　　　　　　　　　　　　　　　mom
　　　　　　　　　　　　　　　1/31/06

10

My grandmother, my father's mother, who cared for me at Sunnyhills, used her Korean name, Kang, and kept another unknown to everyone. My grandmother took me to the Lion Market to see its double-stacked fish tanks collect sludge on their purple glass. We returned, crossing the sheet-metal-covered parking lot and passing into the shade of our doorway, where late at night, my mother appeared, saying, "If I kiss you and hold you in my arms, how would your grandmother feel?" Only a mother can push away her own child. During the day, my grandmother rolled up her long skirt like a hand of noodles and set out *unagi-don* on a fold-out table. I listened to her footsteps in leather moccasins, walking under the plum trees; she wore an embroidered vest, camphor wafting out from the patches for arthritic pain she let me put on her wrists and back. We delivered batches of *inarizushi* to the other grandmothers. Never was she anything other than what I have described—never a young woman or a small girl until she told me years later her name.

One day I overheard her speaking strangely inside Yaohan Plaza at the sushi counter to the packing ladies. She never talked in this manner with the other grandmothers, or with her children and grandchildren. Her hands expressed shock; the packing ladies nodded, taken by intrigue. Their exchange was alluring, then pleading and jesting, with a ricochet of smiles. But my grandmother would not teach me Japanese. She heard with concern the words I could understand and speak. *Usagi*. Rabbit. Her impulse was to secure me with English, my troublesome tongue but one I depended on to survive. Her insistence must have hidden a longing or loneliness, for there were days upon days that she did not speak Japanese. The way I had heard her talking seemed almost imaginary. Those Sunday mornings when my mother was too exhausted to take us to Yaohan Plaza.

~

In 1923, Shinjuku, my grandmother Kumiko was born Japanese. She was born the year of the Great Kantō Earthquake that reduced Tokyo to ashes. False rumors of Koreans poisoning wells, looting, and mobilizing emerged that afternoon in Yokohama and Kawasaki and spread to the

northernmost island of Hokkaido. She was born the year
of the ensuing Kantō Massacre. Japanese mobs armed with
swords and bamboo spears murdered six thousand Koreans.
Children's necks sliced open. Parents nailed down, tortured.
Bodies like fish stacked onshore. To pass as Japanese, they
asked survivors to say what the Korean tongue betrayed—a
price: "15 yen, 50 sen." *Jugo en, goju ssen.*

In Korean, *Chugo en, gochu ssen.*

"15 yen, 50 se—"

"15 yen, 5—"

"15 yen, 50 sen—"

"15 ye—"

"15 yen, 50 sen," her father said quickly.

Her mother, with a two-week-old Kumiko, said, "15
yen, 50 sen."

A decade later, for school, her family moved seven miles
east to Ueno, where Kumiko never asked for anything. She
skipped through white blossom curtains of sakura trees, over
slatted bridges toward Ueno Zoo. The zoo housed exotic
animals from around the world. The handsomest leopards,
the longest snakes, parades of bears and elephants. She was
nineteen when the officials, fearing the wild beasts might
escape the zoo during an air attack, and wanting to con-
serve the supplies being used to keep them alive, ordered the
beasts to be killed by poisoning, starvation, or other means.
It did not feel like war until the posters listed air-raid drills
and numbers upon numbers of dead beasts. For her and her
classmates, it was their first experience of fear.

In the dim light of her room, her mother and father confessed that she was Korean. They had been forced to leave Jeju Island after their country was annexed by Japan. They had changed their language; their names, long erased; and their manners, learned. For appearances, they were educators. They had never said anything before, and if Kumiko had suspected it, she did not say. The trouble with hiding is that either you are found before you are killed, or you are killed before you are found—death hides you forever.

Kumiko left Ueno with her parents, bringing with her a recollection of her homeroom. One morning, years ago, she saw the shadows of her classmates who had already seated themselves—the soft ways in which they adjusted their delicate arms over their desks. Kumiko's teacher, standing over her in a pleated skirt, lifted her hands from Kumiko's eyes. Kumiko let herself adjust to the brightness. She faced the large windows. The room appeared to rock with the blinds that jostled left and right, playing light across her vision. Well-wishes for her birthday hung on green strips of paper across the windows of her homeroom: *a new cake, a happy life, a big family, a magic spell, a sea urchin, a song.* Even after she had learned of her history, Kumiko would always belong in Ueno, at least within that private place where one puts away her most precious memories.

Jeju Island was the least private place she had ever known. An island with a plentitude of rocks, wind, and women. Matriarchal, she had heard, throughout centuries, and led by *haenyeo*, Sea Women. In home-knitted wet suits, girded with knives, Sea Women dove thirty meters below the black waves. Once they descended, they were neither saved nor called upon to return. For three minutes, Sea Women were beyond human. They lived practically underwater, each body muscled and tough. They kicked their pale legs, trailing their ponytails like fins on their heads, and surfaced a bounty they had harvested for the islanders to sell, trade, and cook: abalone, conch, octopi, oysters, sea urchins, and more. Lauded for holding air inside their cells, for their litheness of movement, detailed orientation, eyes unblinking in the violent sea, softer fats with higher thresholds in cold water, and hearts suited for the dive, they crested above water and into the golden shawl of the sun as deities. Sea Women married men who gave them girls for diving.

Kumiko wondered how she could fit in with them. When had she last held her breath? Her toes split open when she trod on volcanic rocks. The other girls, as young as eleven, submerged themselves into icy waters. The men's faces were the color of boiled chicken after forgoing meals to feed their broad-shouldered, lean-muscled wives and daughters. When the girls crowded the dirt roads, they raced one another to the reefs. Their shirts hung around their waists, and their dark-haired backs, tanned bodies stirred intimidation into the islanders, at once powerless and proud, as one might feel peering into the dark water or the black eyes of children.

Kumiko and her parents were welcomed. Nobody could say why exactly. Her family name would change when she married another islander. Her children would be descendants of one of three ancient founders: Koh, Bu, and Yang. The islanders also remembered her parents from a long time ago, remembered their mothers and fathers. Kumiko learned, through the islanders, the measure of what generosity ought to be.

Kumiko loved the islanders. They were different from the people of Ueno, who put on a show of ignorance to save face, and the faces of others, out of prudence. Chastisement was subtle: a frown, a gaze. Some might have preferred it if they were told it was a righteous upbringing. On Jeju Island, mothers publicly embraced fathers, a normally sacred contact between lovers. Kumiko preferred the wildness of the islanders. Their faces showed the contempt of empty nets. Their eyes cut into her. Their slick words and heavy fists. They never let Kumiko wonder where she stood with them. They taught her how to talk over the roar of the sea. They shouted at her, kissed her, scolded her, praised her, and the whole island, together, expected the world of her—to see, to know, and to provide.

~

At the outbreak of the military campaign, Kumiko's father could not be sure what the campaign would bring. South Korean police forces, backed by the United States, encircled the island. The police began to carry out civilian executions. They were looking for spies, but partway through, they killed anybody. At night, extreme anti-Communist and Communist groups, fueled by resentment, killed islanders indiscriminately. Kumiko's father, whose knowledge came from a lineage of archers and horse tamers, understood he could not fight, not here; he must run. For months, he had read headlines steeped in mistrust: FREE AND INDE-PENDENT KOREA and KOREAN COMMUNIST PARTY and REJECTED PEOPLE'S REPUBLIC OF KOREA and MILITARY CAMPAIGN AGAINST LEFT-WING INSUR-GENTS and ILLEGAL TO CROSS BETWEEN NORTH AND SOUTH LINES. The country sliced down the middle like a walnut cake.

Among the islanders, Kumiko's father overheard, "Free? We're not free. Our military? Trained by the Japanese, controlled by the Americans. The North Korean leader? A real Soviet. A campaign on our island? Who do they think they are, to slaughter their own brothers?"

"You say mainland Koreans see us as brothers?" somebody said, laughing. "They see us as shit. They only enjoy getting rid of us because they were *told* we were shit."

Other islanders hoped, saying, "They won't split up Korea. The Japanese put all the industry in the North. They left all the agriculture in the South. North and South? We need each other. You cut a rabbit in half and you lose the legs, or you lose the head, then you don't have a rabbit anymore. Let the idiots realize it soon."

With no uncertainty that the campaign would breach their shores, the islanders gathered their families and hunted for hideouts. The first to be executed protested outside their homes. "I'd rather be shot here than bayoneted while hiding in the bushes!"

Protesters shouted for reunification and independence. Thousands of forces landed on Jeju to end the opposition quickly, root out islanders from house to house.

The water touched low on the cliffs. Kumiko's father watched his daughter, who had surprised the islanders with her irrepressible spirit. Her hair and eyes filled with the light of the sea in front of her. He noticed her looking for the women who had jumped off the cliffs to their deaths. She scanned the deeper waters until her concern grew into the size of an adult.

Kumiko's family ran to a shack in the mountainside where they would not be seen. Burial mounds, like people under blankets, left shadows along the mountain to protect them during the day. Her father had kept them from bringing anything, not even photographs. Nobody could comfort her mother, who wept and lamented. Her father could not reassure them of their own safety, and his silence was enough to suggest the dangers they would face. The fires had started.

"We can't stay here doing nothing," her mother said. "We always run, why do we have to run?"

For the first time, Kumiko cursed her. "Mother, stop talking crazy."

Her mother said, "I'm the only *human* here. Think about your aunts and uncles. We have to bring them to safety."

"We'll be found out, lugging people all the way up here," Kumiko said. "They won't make it. What about the killings, the smoke? Do you want us to die, too?"

"Let me go then," her mother said. "I'll go myself. You're a coward like your father."

Her father said to her mother, "You won't make it there and back."

"She's lost her mind," Kumiko said, but her father quieted her.

"You don't believe me," her mother said to him, "but I'll go fetch them myself."

"You'll die for sure," he said. "And if the others are safe, you'll endanger *them*."

"I won't listen to a man who only saved himself."

During the night, her father decided to leave the mountain. Kumiko begged him not to go. It was clear to her that he was doing it to soothe her mother's anxieties. Her father did not expect to find any others, though he would try, and at least he could bring back news. It was true that they knew nothing of what was going on. They watched the fires, smelled the smoke. Kumiko cried, "How can she let you go down the mountain? If you don't come back, I won't forgive her, and I won't forgive you." Startled at her own harsh words, she added, "Don't leave us here alone."

Her father embraced her. "Don't say such things," he said, and warned her about the antics between husbands and wives. Even during war, these things never go away. This made him laugh for the first time in a long while. That was why he depended on his kindhearted daughter. "And your mother is right," he said to her. "We have been running away for too long. Do you understand?"

Then he was gone.

Kumiko and her mother waited for days. It was evident that fires continued to burn the villages. It could only mean there was still danger down below. Her mother reassured her, "He's waiting for the right time to slip away. He's helping someone. We can't just think of ourselves."

Hungry and frightened, they clung to each other at night. If they heard a rustle nearby, it could be her father—or the police or the groups of men.

Rocking back and forth, Kumiko thought back to the long afternoons, algae cresting the sea's surface, buoys attached to the girls' waists. Jeju was an island in abundance of rocks, wind, and women. You could go in any direction, and you would find only these three things. Now, whether she faced north or south, east or west, there was only fire.

When Kumiko and her mother came down the mountain, the island was scorched. They passed through burnt villages, their voices lodged in their throats. Many of the dead could not be found, their bodies tossed over cliffs, hidden away in caves, or chopped into bits—signs of covering up. Mothers cupped the air with their hands, holding the missing faces of their husbands and sons. Their wailing and screaming filled the hearts of all who sifted through the remains. Teeth. Hair. Dead horses and pigs, then mosquitoes. The smoke reddened the sun. They covered their mouths, or they would taste the corpses. There were children, the girls Kumiko played with, and women and men, lying with limbs bent over each other, splayed across the road. Tens of thousands of them, idle along collapsed terraces where the islanders once danced, pumping with life.

It was Kumiko who crossed the road, over a bridge, and came to a part of the ground soaked in blood. When she asked after her father, somebody pointed to this ground. She saw nothing except the many faces around her, mouths wide and sullen.

One islander, a grandmother, said to her, "Your father was captured at the bottom of the mountain and dragged into a demonstration." She explained that a demonstration was a public display. A group of men, unfed and irate, corralled a crowd together. They put on such displays on behalf of the country, and on higher orders, forgoing restraint. What evil was born out of demonstrations?

"Then where is he?" Kumiko asked.

The grandmother opened her palm toward the ground. "Here."

Looking closer, flesh and bone, gristle mistaken for bark and debris between the stones. At once, the road became vivid and Kumiko recognized her father:

(Road) (Father) (Road)

"They stoned him until he was gravel," the grandmother said, as though she were not speaking to Kumiko but a deity who had come down from the mountain to judge her for the truth. "Many of us stoned him to prove our innocence. We stoned our own, again and again."

They stoned him over nights. They pitched blunt rocks harder, over days, for sport, until finally boredom, before the body was pulverized. What was exchanged between the police and the groups of men and the islanders, between the rocks and the bones? Between the body and the road? What was supposed to be understood? Though they did not know it, the days that Kumiko and her mother spent hiding on the mountain were given a name.

Such were the questions raised by the Jeju Island Massacre of April 3, 1948.

~

Kumiko ran—to Daejeon, South Korea, and had children with her husband, a six-foot, hulking man, who opened the country's first insurance company and drank away his earnings. He beat her, at times mercilessly, and she accepted it. If her father had done the same to her mother, then he would still be alive. Her mother stayed behind in Jeju.

Two years later, when Kumiko was twenty-seven, the Korean War broke out. North Korean soldiers came to Daejeon, executed its civilians. South Korean soldiers arrived and shot the survivors, in fear of defectors. Kumiko understood that she must perfect her Korean. Her husband taught her how to erase her Japanese tongue.

Still, she was not a slave. No soldier risked touching a woman with the enteric signs of typhoid fever affecting eighty thousand. Ancient outbreaks ravaged the country:

typhus, scarlet fever, dysentery, smallpox, Japanese enceph-
alitis. A cholera epidemic put ten thousand out of fifteen
thousand infected to rest. Quarantine was impossible. No
structure for vaccines existed. Kumiko watched the American soldiers, so close to death, fondle the crosses hanging
from their necks. The heavy rain and neglected corpses invited mosquitoes, infecting all others with malaria. Most
of all, suspicion was infectious. American soldiers gunned
down terrified refugees under a railroad bridge because they
could not tell anybody apart. There were the many flags of
soldiers from different countries who had come to fight,
whose flags Kumiko could not even tell apart.

She hid money in the folds of her clothes and slept in her
dusty robes she wore during the day. She was not in one of
the hundreds of groups that died protesting. She was not in
hell. Hell was up north, where American planes were carpet-
bombing, sending sticky fire into towns. Orphans emerged
with charred skin and gooey fish eyes, or were baked upon
the pockmarked lands. Their bodies, smeared into shadows,
left wrinkles on the face of the earth.

She had not been in Japan when the bombs fell, and she
would survive the violent division of her country. Amid war,
disease, she gave birth to six children.

Kumiko hardly spoke to her mother. In Kumiko's heart,
her mother's sense of responsibility, her thoughts of those aunts
and uncles and other families, had killed her father. Only once
did Kumiko confront her mother when she visited Daejeon.
Kumiko was caring for her youngest, her six-year-old son, my

father, when she voiced her accusations against her mother. Her mother fell to the floor, sobbing. The sight must have punished Kumiko because she never neglected her mother again. After leaving an island stewarded by women and girls, Kumiko said, "I have headstrong sons and a powerful husband." But when she sought out her mother's filled grave, placed in a Daejeon cemetery apart from the island and closer to Kumiko, she waited for something—a supernal light or an unordinary voice. After completing the ancestral rights, she felt what was explicit at last between them. She said to her mother, "I am still so mad." Kumiko touched the grave like a door she could enter. "But not at you."

With slow, arthritic fingers, she covered her upright body in layers of winter coats, ones she could not afford in her youth. Her eyes unblinking as she nestled me into her arms. She had followed her son and his wife and their son to this country. She could not be sure what living in America would bring. However, watching over me, her youngest grandchild, in Milpitas, my grandmother must have felt the urge to teach me how to sing in Korean. *San*, mountain. *Toki*, rabbit. "Listen carefully," she said, and sang with deep resonance a children's verse. "Dear mountain rabbit, where are you going? Hopping as you *run* and *run* away, where do you think you're going?"

~

I wondered about her speaking with the Korean grandmothers and the Japanese sushi-counter ladies. When

I began school, she wanted to read and write in English. Every night, she asked me to write an English phrase for her in her notebook. She would then copy it in large, neat handwriting. One night, I was eager to get to bed. In the morning, my grandmother had finished her stretches and exercises. She was watering her garden out front. Looking at her notebook, I saw the last few pages were empty because I had not given her any words the night before. I remember it so clearly because she would not ask for them again.

When my grandmother passed, she left a sum of money for my mother, and a note that she did not leave such a sum to any other, because my mother had paid, as Kumiko had paid, as her own mother had paid—in spite of damage, desperation, and terror—for their responsibilities, between a daughter-in-law and a mother-in-law, as mothers who were no longer daughters, as daughters who had lost their mothers. But my grandmother was a woman who felt the blunt force of a fist harder than anyone. After a blood test, we learned that I was part Japanese. My mother dismissed her parents, Jun and Lee. She said they could only be Korean. My parents pointed at Kumiko's mother or Kumiko for the Japanese part of our family. Maybe there was a violence we did not know about. Kumiko could have been a Japanese woman who became a Korean one.

When she lay on her hospital bed, the joy she let in was the joy in meeting her mother and father again. She recalled the Jeju spring hills, covered in tracts of yellow canola—golden and mystical as the fragrant blooms traveled down and across field upon field. The volcano crater in the backdrop was striking against the closer azaleas, the profusion of cherry blossoms springing from white to pink, orange to red. Cooking competitions sprouted at the ports, programs to enrich prayers for harvest, and from her memory of the farms, riding lessons with native horses, known for their larger heads and thick necks, coats of chestnut, cream, sorrel, some silver-gray with a long mane, and others with freckles and hairless ankles and spotted noses.

Despite her longing, Kumiko chose to rest in California. Her grave was cleared of weeds pulled by the workers she had greeted herself the previous year. Maybe she wanted to be close to her family, buried in the country chosen by her children. As I learned Japanese, roamed through Ueno and the elevator of that ryokan, I learned to isolate myself through language—from English to Korean to Japanese. It was so effective it was frightening, as if I could guard against others like a spy. Where I could hardly open my mouth before, it now seemed that no one could speak to me. Languages, as they open you, can also allow you to close. When I felt myself running toward seclusion, I heard my grandmother and my great-grandfather urging me to try—and how much harder one must try when learning to love. She never asked me to speak but to understand, rather than endure to forgive, and never to sacrifice, only to let go.

11

Hello? Eun Ji,

Mommy came home last night. Because it snowed so much, Mommy, Auntie, and the others, five altogether, played in Icheon instead. Spending lots of time with Auntie from Daejeon makes me happy. I recall there's only one year left before I go back and I'm sorry I won't see Auntie like this anymore. Now it's almost about time the cold stops and Spring arrives, but yesterday, it snowed anyway.

These days, I haven't been able to meet with Gwi Won. Mommy's been a bit busy, you know. Your Little Uncle from Daejeon has moved. To a smaller house. Still, it's a relief he moved at all. I've got to spare some time and stop by. If I see the house, I might become disheartened. But I should go, shouldn't I?

How's Eun Ji doing? Your brother sounds very *stressed*. The *sewer line* in the backyard exploded, so he can't go to work. He kept shouting, "The housework is going to kill me." While talking to you on the phone, your brother said he had something to tell me, too. After you went outside with *Aeson*, I talked to *John*. The truth is Mommy was so guilty that she couldn't say anything. I'm curious if everything got fixed all right. After I post this letter, I'll try giving you guys a call. I'm sorry to Eun Ji, too. For now, all I can do is wait for the two of you to graduate. At least that's what it seems like.

When I visit in March, I'll have to discuss what to do next. Nothing comes easy in life, they say. (*Free*) things are even rarer. I get what I give, (*It's payback for what I did*), and if there are hard times, there are also good times. And when there is money, there are times of spending, right? That's living. So they say there's nothing to be heartbroken or sad about. Because that's how (*life*) has always been.

It's time for Mommy to head out. You know Hee Jung? She got married last year. She had a baby and told me to come today to see it. I'm supposed to go with Hoya. Mommy's head is scattered so I wanted to stay home, but I promised them last week, you know. Even when I played with Auntie and the others, Mommy's heart flew off to *Davis*. I want to hurry over and do all sorts of things for you, so my heart aches. As I leave the house, I'll try giving you a call.

Eun Ji, you don't have any news, do you? Last time, your friend who lied to you, what a joke. Of all the things in life! Anyway, it's a good lesson. Now, you know there are people like that. Laughable. During the week, be well and have fun with your life. Mommy will think long and hard for a couple days. On *Monday*, I'll write again. Bye.

Mom
February 10, 2006

안녕? 은지

엄마는 어젯밤에 돌아왔어.

눈이 너무 많이 와서 이천에서 이모들 하고

다섯명이 놀았어.

대전 이모 하고 시간을 많이 보내서 너무 좋아.

이제 1년만 있으면 간다고 생각하니까

이모 하고 자주 못 만나는것도 아쉽단다.

이제는 그만 춥고 봄이 올 때가 되가는데

어제도 눈이 왔어.

요즘에는 규원이 아줌마랑 잘 못만나.

엄마가 좀 바빴거든.

대전 삼촌은 이사했어. 좀 작은집으로.

그래도 이사 해서 다행이지 뭐.

시간내서 한 번 가봐야지.

보면 속상할것도 같지만 그래도 가봐야겠지?

은지는 어떻게 지내?

오빠는 stress가 많은것 같드라.

마당에 ～～ sewer line 터졌다고 일도 못가고

집안일이 너무 많아 죽겠다면서 막 소리지르더라.

너랑 전화 하다가 창현이가 할 말 있다고 해서

너는 aeson 하고 나가고 나서 John 이랑

통화 했거든.

사실 엄마가 미안해서 뭐라고 막 못했어.

다 고쳤는지 궁금하다.

편지 보내놓고 전화 해볼꺼야.

은지 한테도 미안하고.

일단은 둘다 ※ 졸업하길 기다릴 수 밖에는

별도리가 없구나.

3월에 가면 앞으로 어떻게 할지
의논을 좀 해야겠어.
세상에 쉬운 일이 없단다.
공짜 (free)는 더욱 더 없구.
내가 한 만큼 돌아오고, 어려울때가 있으면
좋을때가 있지.   It's paid back what I did
돈도 생기면 쓸데가 있고, 그치?
사는게 그래.
그래서 너무 속상해 하거나 슬퍼할것이 없단다.
삶 (life)이란 는 그런거니까.
엄마 이제 나가봐야 할 시간이다.
희정이 오나 알지?
작년에 결혼 했거든.
아기 낳았다고 오늘 보러오래.
은아하고 같이 가보기로 했어.
엄마 머리속이 복잡해서 집에 있고 싶은데
지난주에 약속을 미리 해놨거든.
이모들 하고 놀면서도 엄마 마음은 Davis 에
가 있었어.
얼는 가서 이것저것 해주고 싶은데 마음이 아프다.
나가면서 전화 해봐야지.
은지는 별일 없는거지?
지난번 그 거짓말 한 친구는 정말 웃긴다.
세상에 별일이다!
어쨌든 좋은 경험이야
그런애들도 있다는걸 알았으니까. 웃겨.
주말에 잘 지내고 즐겁게 살도록 해.
엄마도 며칠 잘 생각하고 월요일에 다시 쓸께.

안녕   2006. 2. 10. Friday monday
                                mom.

12

In my second year of college, when I was visiting Bundang during the winter, I left in the night for an audition in Yongsan, north of the Han River. Deep inside an
entertainment company, concrete hallways led to a dance
studio with polished floors and practice mirrors. Bora,
a trainee and a school friend of mine, had invited me in
for a solo audition. She chatted with her manager, David,
who was in his forties with soft gray eyebrows. David was
hired to clean up the poor relationship between trainees
and the company. A debuted group of teenage boys lined
up against the wall, pointing at my parka over my hoodie
and baggy jeans. Nobody was safe from their scrutiny. The
head of the company kept to himself in the corner—a man
in a loose-fitting suit called Hee Chul.

They did not dim the lights. The room was dark already. Silhouettes mingled across the floor. Outside, hail pelted the windows. The room's speakers buzzed on. Everyone stopped talking.

"It's a smaller company," David said to me, and cupped his hands together. "We don't have the connection that bigger places do with the broadcasting companies."

Hee Chul took a pack of cigarettes out of his suit pocket. "No one can pull you any favors," he said, "not even *me*. Bora's told you already?"

Bora nodded at him. Only a year of her training had passed, and the company already pushed for her debut in a five-member girl group. Other trainees were considered for the open spots, but David and Hee Chul hoped for somebody new.

The boys' pale, delicate faces hung in the air. Though they had debuted, they were not on a schedule of variety shows and performances. Hee Chul added, "It's our fault. Whatever you grasp too tightly, you lose. We hired the best choreographer and the best vocal coaches." He took another drag. "It takes years to get a group ready, but only a few seconds for people to decide whether they will love you or let you die."

"This girl group will be different," David said quickly to Hee Chul. "There's nothing like it in Korea. We're better than a lot of those companies anyway. They already sold out in a sleazy industry. Plus, we have Bora, 'the leader.' The rest of the spots will fill automatically. We need 'the youngest,' 'the dancer,' 'the vocal,' and 'the visual'—"

"Can we hear you sing?" Hee Chul asked me.

"I'm not a singer," I said.

Hee Chul laughed. "I have bad luck," he said. "It's not your fault." He folded his arms. "Let's talk about something. Bora said you're on a dance crew in California."

~

In my first year in Irvine, California, I had auditioned for a competitive hip-hop dance crew that performed forty times a year and once at the House of Blues in West Hollywood. The dance crew won first in regionals and placed in international competitions. On the West Coast, you hoped to join a crew. Anyone could audition if they showed. Three hundred candidates waited under the stadium bleachers for their number to be called. The crowd stood over terraced seats. Phones in the air recorded dancers on the floor.

A young man with a news camera panned the stadium. The girl beside him pointed at the number pinned on my shirt and shouted, "Good luck—hope you kill it."

She saw the confusion on my face.

"Oh honey," she explained. "Like crush it, slaughter it, *murder* it."

The young man asked me, "What's your background? Cheer squad?"

I had never seen a cheer squad before.

Those candidates who had performed admirably sat in the dirt outside, sharing a cigarette that glowed as it passed from hand to hand. On the faces of those who performed poorly, a grief meant for a small room. Those still waiting disappeared into the corners to go over the routine again. I did this with my nightmares. When I woke up, I would go over my dream the way I wished it had gone.

Looking around, the audition appeared to have been put together without a plan. One brought a table. Another set up the speakers. The judges carried in their own chairs.

I would never forget the choreographers' voices during the practice run: "Get your mermaid-ass hair on the floor!" "When you lick your hand, don't fake it. You *lick* it." "Book it offstage." "Facials!" "Boom, boom, *cack*." "Pop, pop, *melt*." "It's a cack, not a tic." Any motion equaled a sound in the throat. And those whose lives were filled with excitement could only go looking for it to the lengths of chaos.

The judges called me down to the floor with two others. They told us that we competed for more than a crew. They were a family that cared for you.

We danced three at a time. You had to look up when you performed the routines because your facial expressions mattered. Once you looked down, the stands would go quiet. You should never hear yourself breathe.

The crowd was like openmouthed corvinas in a water tank. They watched for one of us to slip or topple over. We each hoped it would not be us. The other two candidates, in my periphery, stared at the judges. I looked up at the crowd and held them in contempt, with a sense of accusation, exposing them to my longing and fears. What pleasure could match the feeling of one's pounding heart? I could bleach my hair, lengthen it with extensions, sharpen my nails, and wear tight black clothes during a time when being naked was not enough. I vowed that I would no longer withhold or force up food, so I was allowed by some miracle to move in the body I had neglected.

Screams filled the stadium as we walked off the floor.

~

"I'm on a dance crew," I said to Hee Chul with pride. "It's my second year. We just got back from a competition in Los Angeles."

"You've got to take those pictures down," Hee Chul said to me. "Bora already showed me. Your arms and legs and chest are showing."

I offered, "We're all dressed the same."

"Don't be so stern," David said to him.

"People won't like this," Hee Chul said, ashing his cigarette into a soda can on a desk. "It's too scandalous for a debut girl group." He sounded panicked.

Bora set up a song on a disc player. She was ready to play music.

"Hold on," David said to her, then turned to me. "Are you willing to move here?"

"I have *family* here," I said.

"That's what my mother would say. Sometimes you sound like an American," David said, and patted my back. "Other times, you're just like a Korean."

The boys, maybe seven all together, stood idly. After six years of training, each had been picked from a pool of a hundred trainees. The others had been discarded. Bora had described the lonely and despondent life of a trainee. Suffering is trusted to shape one's skills and spirit. The mistake trainees make is not realizing that a debut is another grueling competition against other debut and senior groups.

I said to David and Hee Chul, "I'm supposed to be here."

Hee Chul smiled at me. "You don't even speak to me like I'm older than you. It's rude and clumsy, but it's also refreshing."

David got up and paced the floor. "You know your weight?"

I gave him a number that was five pounds lighter.

"What's that in kilograms?" David asked Bora. She mouthed the number.

"You're heavier than you look," Hee Chul frowned. "It's heavy for Korea. The girls here are smaller and lighter. A girl should be a sheet of paper."

David glared at Hee Chul. "Don't listen to him," David said to me. "We'll start with fifteen pounds. When you shed the weight, your face will start to change."

Hee Chul smoked again, used the cigarette to scratch his nose. "Everyone has a story."

"She knows Japanese," David said. "It's the right market for us."

"This is good." Hee Chul pointed the cigarette at David, who stood taller. "She's a lighthearted girl. She's never lived in Korea. She needs help getting along and she gets a lot wrong. She shakes your hand when she should bow. But over time, she grows on you and she starts to get some things right. She even teaches you a few things about honesty."

"And not so pretty that other girls will feel hatred toward her," David said. "She can be your best friend."

"For the boys," Hee Chul said. "She's their friend, too."

"Are you sure?" David asked.

"She's a tomboy but she surprises you. You know that sensation. When you realize you've fallen in love with your friend, and you see her as a girl for the first time?"

"It's transformative," David considered. "That should happen after the debut—"

"You come out of the blue," Hee Chul said.

"That's the moment, isn't it?" David said to himself.

"Maybe you'll need to lose a little more than fifteen pounds," Hee Chul said to me. "When you think you can't lose any more, think about how orphans steal when they're hungry. You can do anything if you need to."

"Hee Chul," David said. "Shrinking can age you, can't it?"

"She's not young," Hee Chul said. "But that's okay."

"We won't push it," David said to me. "Hee Chul's the real deal. He just sounds coarse, but he wants you to succeed. We can't succeed without each other. You have to be strong because this industry is always going to be dirty and unfair."

"Don't forget about Hyerin, or was it Hyeri," Hee Chul said.

"What happened to her?" I asked.

Bora, who had been quiet, said, "She works somewhere else now."

"Doing what?" I asked.

Hee Chul finished his smoke and offered one to David, who declined.

"What happened to her is on her," David said. "Your fate is in your hands."

Hee Chul seemed hurt, but the look vanished from his face. "Let's see you dance."

~

After I had been asked to join the dance crew, I dialed one person to share the news. When the call rang, I closed my eyes and saw his labored smile during our final weeks together. He would sneak me a cigarette if he knew I could not sleep. He asked me questions about our future until I said that I would save my cigarette for a later hour. He would then throw his arms up, say that he would save his with me. In 1984, one year after Lee's death, my mother had given birth to my brother. She had washed his naked body in a red tub on a roof somewhere, alone, without her parents and without my father. My brother was her only delight. "But she has this smile on her face," my brother once said to me, describing a picture of them on that roof. "She needed me just as much as I needed her."

With my brother, I had wondered what would happen to us, and whether anyone would believe even the good parts. It was not common for a young man like him to prepare a Thanksgiving dinner, pick up the sides, lay out a honey-baked ham, and coax his friends over for their laughter. Aeson ran in circles. Mieko chipped off husks of millet. We played video games together because we, as brother and sister, had come from the same place, and that was the place we longed for, which united us. Such realizations came harder to those who could not embrace each other from time to time. When something was a mystery, it also became a thing to wonder. I watched the sun stand on its legs and I turned eighteen.

Months had passed since I last heard or saw him when he picked up the phone. "Eun Ji?" he answered. "Don't worry about me. Are you doing better now?"

~

Bora dropped me off at my parents' apartment in Bundang. My mother swung open her metal door upon hearing my foot-steps in the hall. Her cotton face mask had peeled off during her sleep, hanging onto her chin. Then I told her everything.

"Are you sure?" she asked, suddenly awake. "I don't know anybody else on television except for Gwi Won's daughter. Oh my God, I have to tell somebody."

We looked up the company website together. She read through the paper contract given to me. We called my brother, and he sounded in awe.

"What do you think?" I asked my mother. "I can move here and live with you. I'll go to international school. I can be a trainee and take the subway to the studio."

"What about Irvine? You have friends there. You started your life already."

"Are you listening?" I asked her. "I can be here with you—"

"Don't misunderstand. I want you to come, but—"

"But what?"

"You were born there. That's your home," she said. "You don't know what it's like to live here. It's a very different place with different people."

"I have something to do here," I said in shock. "I can do a good job."

My father came home later that night. He was exhausted but happy to read my contract. He asked me to give him a day or two to find out more about the company and the industry before I signed. He explained to me there was a lot of talk about everything that went on in this country. One of his old colleagues from Daejeon was the head of a broadcasting company. "When you live here, everybody knows who you are, which family you belong to, and what you've done wrong," he said.

The next day, my father came home after work. He ate his rice, drank his soup, and left to brush his teeth and change into his pajamas. He lay on a pad in front of the TV eating snacks and surrounded by floor pillows. My mother and I ordered chicken wings later in the night, and after they were delivered, we chewed the gristly parts together.

The day after, my father returned late. After dinner, he sat on the couch, and my mother and I waited for him to speak. He had met with the colleague he had mentioned to me, the head of the broadcasting company. My father asked what would happen if his daughter were to debut with a girl group. The man said I would be fortunate to debut, one of thousands, but I needed sponsors to gather interest and would be indebted to old men.

The man bragged that he slept with young girls regularly, and to his credit, told my father the truth. The man bet that he would eventually sleep with me.

"What about Bora?" my mother asked me.

I said, "She's already signed on—"

"Go home," my mother said to me. "You're not safe here. And we'll come back to you after our next contract—"

"Your *next* contract?" I asked her.

"We've signed on for two more years," she said. Counting the years from their first two contracts, they would be gone for seven years all together. "Now I know it was the right choice to leave you." She grabbed my suitcase and started to pack my clothes. "Forget about being a trainee. If it was the right thing for you, then it would have happened."

My father was so furious at the man that he nearly assaulted him but remembered he had asked him for a favor.

~

Meeting Bora at a coffee shop in the department store in Bundang, I wanted to tell her first and in person. The barista brought us blankets and a candle for the table. "You don't have to say anything," Bora said. "I thought I could keep

going if we did it together. I thought it could work. But I've
wanted to leave for a long time. I tell David that it's getting
too hard, and he keeps telling me the same thing. Be stronger
because this industry—"

"This industry is dirty and unfair," I said.

The barista brought us our coffees and a waffle to share.
"I still want to dance. It's too hard to give up," Bora said. The
barista snuck a glance at her petite frame and face. "Hee Chul's
been calling me. He's different now. He's losing his mind."

"Does he have your number?"

"Of course he does. The company's losing money. He's
drinking a lot. They have to do something. They're getting
desperate. They beat the boys with sticks," she said. "But the
beating is still not as bad as the bigger companies. The boys
are grateful, you know?"

I asked her, "You're going to stay for your debut, right?"

"I could have gone to a bigger company actually," she
said quickly. "But they make you train for too long, and only
three trainees out of three hundred will debut. You won't get
paid until you've been working for five to ten years." She
rocked in her chair. "Last week, this girl group debuted with
our concept. They're all dancers, and they're good."

"I'm sorry—"

She waved her hand. "Don't be," she said. "I actually
got new offers from some companies. They want to give me
contracts, but they want something else, too."

"I don't understand," I said. "What do you do if you
only want to dance or sing?"

"You give it up, or you give up something else," she said, unnerved. "Either way, you'll think about it for the rest of your life—what you *could* have been!"

"What happens if you leave?" I asked her. "You can come to the States."

She laughed and took a bite out of the waffle. "My company won't release my contract. I'll never be able to sign with another company if I'm under contract," she explained. "That's how they keep you. Hee Chul's already scared I'll leave the country. He wants me to meet up with him, drink with him, talk to people I've never met before."

Bora checked her phone. She got up to leave. We stepped outside the coffee shop, and I asked her, "Is that what happened to Hyerin, or Hyeri?" Passersby stalked her with their eyes, watching her every move as she turned to look at me.

"Hyeri?" she asked. "That's what happens to everybody."

~

After leaving Korea, I returned to Irvine and visited the campus clinic, where I signed up to meet with a psychiatrist twice each week. I had blood tests drawn at an off-campus location before going to see my parents, knowing that when I came back, my mind would not feel quite right, and it was true now, as I entered the clinic to schedule my appointments. The clinician said they would discuss my results by the end of my session.

"You called the office on an emergency line," a woman in a white coat said after she introduced herself as Mindy. "My office is just this way." She led me down a hall and into a room. We sat across from each other at a coffee table. On the table, a miniature waterfall bubbled and whirred every so often to churn the muted sobs from strangers beyond the walls. On a closer look, the sculpture was made from a clear tube, a scaffolding that held it together. The sense of the water falling was an illusion.

"You've had hallucinations," Mindy said, and set a clipboard on her knee.

"Of my grandmother."

"It was only that one time, correct?"

I nodded. "She used to have a name for me."

"She gave you a name?"

"I only told my mother, but she hated it."

Mindy looked up from her clipboard.

"I even quit my dance crew," I said.

"Are you leaving school?"

Laughing, I said, "I don't know what I'm doing here."

In her office, all her clocks were an hour slow.

"I want to say this clearly," Mindy said, "before you make any rash decisions. I don't want you to misunderstand." She scooted forward. "Your blood tests show that you have a harder time with having good feelings," she said. "You can't be happy like regular people, to put it simply. You don't have those good feelings. You're not making enough of them."

"I can't be happy?"

"When you're normal, you feel down. More so than others. And that's okay. You're going to feel down a lot, but that's your normal."

Behind the waterfall, in the loose netting of light, Kumiko appeared at the edge of the room. She adjusted her quilted vest, stepped forward with Mieko perched on her hand.

"It was Fumiko. She called me Fumiko."

"You can't be happy," Mindy said, "but you can be *reasonable*."

Kumiko smiled at me. She would not stop, as though she could see every choice I had made. She swelled at the way I had buried Mieko, walked to the park on a cold night. Kumiko beamed as if she recognized those days I had sat inside a room, silent, doing nothing except feeling hatred toward my brother, eating my mother's shipments, asking for my parents even if they were perfectly fine, and it was I who wanted them to come back for nobody else but me. She watched as I let Byung Ho collapse and she saw that I could not take her to Ueno and that I should have told my brother in the car that I did not want us to die—that we could live better—and that I stayed quiet many other times. Times I had forgotten came to me now; like when a classmate and his friends in Davis groped me between my legs; like when I was sent to the principal's office after I threatened to kill a boy who squinted to look like me; like when an older man with glasses, a family friend from the southern coast of Korea, promised to roast live eels in a barrel of coal, described how hard they banged

against the drum, and he casually glanced at my feet before
his eyes traveled up my knees and higher, above my stomach,
settling at the height of my heart, and maybe I thought it was
beautiful, the soft earth of that country, the sea breeze like
sweet vinegar to soothe bitterness from my life because what
harmed me did not appear to endanger the foggy trees, our
sesame-oiled tongs, our coolheaded smiles; like how it was
my fault that I had cleaned out Mieko's cage thinking it was
one more burden; and how it was I who made my parents
and my grandmother believe I never heard them and it was
I who could not forgive anyone or I who did not try to get
away from where I was and it was I who had put myself inside
a room such as this.

13

Hi. Eun Ji.

You got back from school okay?

Don't be too sad. Mommy is sorry for leaving you so young. Until the *last of my life*, Mommy's heart will ache. And you know, you've always been strong, but *this time*, Eun Ji was crushed. "Mommy's committed a grave (*sin*) against Eun Ji!" Thoughts like this come to mind.

I'm sorry. I'm sorry . . .

Even so, I want you to forgive Mommy, save your energy, and have some fun instead. Eun Ji is having a hard time while Mommy is asking Eun Ji to live brightly, freely, enthusiastically for me. That's selfish *like a wish*, isn't it? Mommy will get back to Korea and write again. Eun Ji will miss me too much. *I want to tell you, "I love. You," and I want to tell God, "Thanks for letting me have my daughter, Angela."*

Eun Ji! *Don't cry when Mom is not with you. Whenever you are lonely or sad, then sleep as you said. Right?* My Eun Ji, you've done great so far. Now, there's not much time left. *Keep it up!* If Eun Ji doesn't enjoy her life, the *last of my life* won't be just sad, but each and every day, I will feel *regret* and it'll be *hell.* Eun Ji is *smarter* than Mommy, *stronger* than Mommy, so Eun Ji can do this for me? Okay? *Please.* Since it's *already* the 15th, *only 2 ½ weeks* until December 3rd. Let's say, "Aja, aja, *fighting!"* Okay?

Eun Ji, Mommy loves Eun Ji a lot, and *personally*, I like Eun Ji. Good-looking, lovable, kind, courageous . . . Down the road, whoever (?) is the one (?) to marry my Eun Ji is a person born with all the luck in the world. Right?

Eun Ji, let's live as diligently as possible. If you want to live to 133 *years*, then you must prepare yourself. Mommy, too, when she goes back to Korea, she'll live earnestly. I will only drink *Coke* when I truly want to, otherwise, I'll restrain myself. Each and every day, I will, for sure, *take a walk* and stay healthy. I'll also study my *Japanese.* My Eun Ji, you too, you must take good care of yourself. You know this, right? Then, let's meet December 18th, *only a month* away. Eun Ji. Bye.

November 15, 2006

1.

Hi. 은지.

학교 잘 갔다 왔어?
너무 슬퍼하지마.
엄마가 너 너무 일찍 떼어 놔서 미안해.
Last of my life 엄마도 늘 가슴 아플거야.
그런데
늘 씩씩 했는데 this time 은지가 너무 많이
슬퍼 하니까 '엄마가 은지한테 큰 죄(sin)를 짓는구나!'
그런 생각이 든다.
미안해. 미안해 ...
그래도 엄마 용서하고 힘내서 잘지내줬음 좋겠어.
은지가 너무 힘든데. 엄마가 은지보고
밝고. 명랑하게. 씩씩 하게 살아달라고 하는건 욕심이지?
                                        like a wish

엄마가 한국에 돌아가서도 편지 할께.
은지가 너무 보고 싶을거야.
I want to tell you. "I love. you" and
I want to tell GOD "Thanks to ~~true~~
     let me have my daughter Angela"
은지 !
don't cry when mom is not with you.
whenever you lonely or sad than sleep
   as you said. right?
우리은지. 지금까지 너무 잘해왔어.
이게 얼마남지 않았어. Keep it up!
만약 은지가 잘지내지 않으면 엄마 last of life 가
슬프게 아니라. 매일매일 regret 하면서 hell 같는거야
은지가 엄마보다 smart 하고 strong 하니까
그래 줄 수 있지? 응? please.
already 15th 니까 12월 3일 까진 only 2½ week
남았어.
우리 "아자아자 Fighting!" 하자. 응?

은지야
엄마는 은지를 너무 사랑하고 ♡
Personly 은지를 좋아해.
이쁘고 사랑스럽고 착하고, 씩씩하고 ...
이다음에 누군지(?) 우리은지랑 결혼하는 놈(?)은
세상에서 제일 복 많은 사람일거야 그치?
은지야.
열심히 살자.
133 years 살아가려면 준비는 해야지.
엄마도 한국에 돌아가서 잘 살게.
Coke은 정말 꼭 먹고 싶을때만 먹고 참을게.
매일 매일 take a walk 하면서 건강하게 지낼게.
Japaness 공부도 열심히 할게.
우리은지도 정말 잘지내야 돼, 알지?
그럼 우리 12월 18일에 만나자.
only a month 남았어.
은지. 안녕

14

Three years. Three years, spring of my junior year. I had
gone to a few classes in the last quarter and had turned in
some assignments, but it was only for show. Not yet summer,
scarves in bright plumage flashed among the students flying
down Ring Road. In her Humanities Hall office, Beatrice, my
school counselor, propped her elbows on her desk and, with
her ring-heavy fingers, slapped the papers. The desk clonked.
The legs shifted. Beatrice stayed still for a while. When she
got up, she opened her windows. The campus trees blew in
the scent of grinds from the coffee shop across the bridge.
"Oh, I got it," she said to me.

"What is it?" I asked.

"A bug." Beatrice stared at her palms. "No, I didn't. Anyway, we need to get you in and out of here, don't we? We've
got to get us out by next year."

The way she said *we*, I felt responsible for the both of us.

"This is where it gets tricky." She whipped her finger across a page. "We are political science majors? But we haven't taken any math requirements?"

"Can I—*we*—still graduate?" I was asking for help.

She smiled. "What do we do?"

"I don't know what to tell us."

"So, you understand." Beatrice pretended to faint on her desk, then sat up in her chair. "Our grades are lower than before. We've got to bring them up to graduate."

"Because they might get lower."

"We can't have that. It'd be trouble for us." She turned toward the window. "We need to complete our requirements. Let's talk about mathematics. *Mathematics*. They call it the highest language. It's the language of God."

"Math?" I said.

She asked me, "What replaces the language of God?"

"Another language?"

"I can't write off this math requirement we have," she said. "It's the one problem keeping us from graduating. But what I can do is replace it."

"Let's do it."

"No, no, no," Beatrice said, skimming course titles.

"*We* can do it together."

Beatrice said, "I got it." She crumpled up a sheet of paper and tossed it into the garbage. On a new sheet, she circled something.

I asked her, "What is it?"

"What replaces the language of *God*?"
I took a breath. "The language of *man*?"
"Poetry," she said.
"What?" I said. "Po-e-try?"
Nodding, Beatrice sat back in her chair.
"Great," I said, feeling excited. "How do you spell it?"

~

I sat myself in the front row of our classroom inside a trailer, or a shipping container docked at the edge of Aldrich Park. I had showered for the first time in two weeks and put on a giant hoodie over jeans, as if going to dance practice. Outside, students loitered on the ramp in the sunlight. Inside, there were mold spores in the carpet. The tiled ceiling had a layer of moisture. The thermostat was broken. The steel jambs on the doors looked as if they would lock us in. On the windows, there were moth wings missing moths. Cockroach legs missing a cockroach. What I thought was a snake skin was a long spool of cobwebs under the chalkboard. Crayons had been crushed underfoot.

The poetry teacher showed up in beach sandals. He was tall enough that he ducked under the doorway. He crossed the trailer in construction pants. When he smiled, a happy double chin appeared. "No need to introduce yourselves," he said quickly. "Let's jump in."

Joe began with a poem called "The Vegetables." The long poem was divided into sections titled after vegetables: "The

Artichoke," "The Asparagus," "The Cauliflower," "Herbs,"
"Corn," "Celery," "Bell Pepper," and "Potatoes." Ignoring the
confused looks of the students, Joe asked the eighteen of us to
read it together, then split us into groups so we could read it
for ourselves. In our groups, we rolled our heads into one neat
opinion about the poem.

Joe stared us down. The room rumbled as we pushed
our tables back together. We argued with each other. Groups
faced off with groups. One boy chucked his shoes and stood
up, out-argued everyone until he was facing off with Joe. The
best part was how Joe took the argument apart. It made us
suspicious of him and of one another.

He never wanted us to think in groups to begin with. Joe
slid his hand under the board, catching cobwebs, then found
a piece of chalk. He was sympathetic to how we insisted on
things we had just learned that afternoon. When Joe directed
his chalk to the board, he ripped this insistence out of our
hands. Now that he had done that, we were not afraid that he
would do it again.

We argued all day and, when I looked outside, the lights
on Ring Road were coming on, one by one. Joe watched us.
He let the clock move.

Korean classroom etiquette places the greatest burden
on the student. If the teacher is cryptic, it is the student's
job to understand. American classrooms burden the teacher,
who is expected to be clear and specific rather than wise.
The students turned on Joe with their frustrations. Joe had
cast us off. Joe had let us get lost.

Time passed so that all the strange things we said between us fit comfortably inside the trailer. It put those things, as I would learn, at an observable distance. The speaker above our heads rang with the bell but no one moved.

Joe said, "You put words together, you make a story."

We agreed with him.

"What about one word?" Joe, who stood in the stratosphere above the desks, continued. "One word has references from history, culture, language—your own experiences and the rest of the world. A single word *is* a story," he said. "When we read a poem, we're not reading one story. We're reading every story at once."

Joe pointed to the poem that was suddenly too large to take on. He described how poets could hold in one poem the whole of human history.

"Can you just tell us?" somebody asked. "What it's supposed to mean?"

Joe frowned. "Supposed to mean?"

"The salad poem."

Joe wiped the screen of his watch. He never resisted the passing of time. Let it come, he seemed to say. Dance used time the same way, drawing attention. "It's not meant to be given to you," he said. "That's why it's a difficult grace."

He reminded us that we had all week to drop the class. He warned us that we had better drop it sooner than later. "If you can't stand not knowing, then you're free to go," he said. "If you don't like the class, no one will make you stay."

The creak of the windows let us know that we were still inside the trailer. For those of us who feared uncertainty, it seemed there was no way into a poem.

Joe said the poem was authored by his own teacher.

He told us about his teacher, his teacher's mother, and the cancer that took her. I read the poem again, shocked, watching a woman who goes into the ground.

"Vegetables?" I asked.

He nodded.

In my room, I took out a sheet of paper and filled it with words. On a second and third, I placed the words in different order. Some words together made no sense but felt as if they ought to. They should know each other, see each other better. I wrote twenty pages before I got up to turn the lights on and returned to my desk.

~

Our class met in the trailer twice a week in the late afternoon. Every day we met, I left only to come back. We had lost a third of our class, who had dropped out on the first day. But those of us who stayed rose from our seats, waited, and listened. Normally the windows steamed, but we opened the door and the wind came in. Toward the end, we lay our foreheads on our desks, lulled to say anything at all, just as we would in the seconds before sleep, until the clip of somebody's voice stirred us:

"Poetry is to say what must be said."

"And nothing more?"

"The truth can't come with tassels—"

"What if the truth is easier with tassels?"

"If you don't want the truth, why read poetry?"

Joe, staring at the thermostat on the wall, opened the lid of his coffee cup and washed the last drops down. "Closer," he said. "What're we doing?"

"We're arguing?"

"We're paying attention," Joe said. Whenever he spoke, his words were sets of clothes that we tried on for ourselves. Sometimes they fit, and other times they were old and baggy. "We're looking up close."

"Everybody can look, can't they?"

Joe took a deep breath. "I don't know. But you have to care. Those of you who've decided to stay and try this out— it's because you care."

The bell rang through the speaker. It was quiet again, and night came out of nowhere. We were surprised to learn we still had our mouths, our legs and arms, our hearts.

I met with Joe at the coffee shop for office hours. He refilled his cup and returned to the table. Nothing seemed as real outside the trailer, and Joe agreed.

He took my papers from me. "Wait—how many poems?"

"I don't know," I said, "maybe forty—"

"When did you write these?"

I almost had not returned after the first day of class. I had been convinced that I would not until I got back to my room.

"You wrote all night," Joe said, laughing. "I wish I could do that." He set his cup down at the edge of the table, so he would not stain the papers. He read through them with a pen in his hand.

Joe asked me, "Is your mom still alive?"

I nodded.

"To be honest," he said, "I don't know how to say this—"

"I'm being mean to her."

"No," he said. "There's no *magnanimity*."

It was my first time hearing the word.

"Do you need proof?"

"What would I do with proof?" Joe cautioned, then he pointed to the page. "Actually, there's somebody who can say it better than me." He gestured to the wall behind me and traced out the shape of the building that lay beyond it. When I looked for myself, he reassured me, "This is your first writing class, isn't it? I'm going to arrange for you to meet the director of the writing program. Her name is Joy, and she won't believe these are your poems."

~

Writing a poem, I came out of absolute darkness. Hundreds of poems I wrote about my mother and grandmother, desperate to write down those who only ever appeared in my head. I hoped for a future with poems and to be alone with them. My mother left voicemails saying she wanted to hear my voice. My roommate knocked on my door, laughing nervously, checking that I was not a dead body. But it was the opposite. At my desk, I felt grateful and alive.

~

I rounded the stairwell to the top floor of a campus building and pushed through a green door into an office where light streamed through a window. In a chair facing the window, Joy was waiting for me. She was middle-aged with short brown hair and pale skin and wore a skirt over riding boots. Her glasses hung from a necklace chain. She must have been thinking deeply because her fingertips arched over her forehead.

"It's quiet," Joy said and motioned for me to take a seat. "I like it since I have to read out loud whatever I put down on paper. You have to hear yourself. Say it in the open. Or you forget you're really *saying* something."

Joy was so quick and her instructions so precise.

"Read everything. Hold it out in front of you, and just go." She touched her throat, and said, "It's here." She tapped my poems on her desk. "Not here."

Joy read one page and I could hear my poem.

"What does your mother call you?" Joy asked me.

"Eun Ji."

"I've been reading your poems," Joy said, pushing away from her desk. She described her daughter to me. She showed me a photograph. In telling me what love felt like to her, she was as careful as anyone could be. "The poems you wrote before are unforgiving," Joy told me. "You don't have to forgive your mother. I'm not telling you to forgive her. But the poem must forgive her, or the poem must forgive you for not. Otherwise, it's not a poem."

"Like magnanimity?" I asked.

She put her hands on the table. "Yes, magnanimity," she said. "You can say anything you want—with magnanimity. We are poets, aren't we?"

"We don't have a lot of things."

"We have poems," she said.

"Do we live on just words?"

"No," she said, laughing. "Nobody can do that."

I asked, "Does a poet have to be reasonable?"

Joy opened a file with my name across the top. "Forgiveness doesn't need a reason. It doesn't follow a logical thought, so it frees you from having to be reasonable."

She shuffled through the first pages. "I'm your adviser from now on," she said. "We are changing your courses and adding the requirements for our department. You must show up and do the work. We have very little time. We're going to stack your quarters. You will be here all summer. There are two or three big awards coming up. You will apply for them today. These poems you have will work. You're interning at the translation center, aren't you? You will meet and learn from poets. Joe knows that you're very good. I know that you can grow. But you can't forget what I'm about to tell you."

I agreed.

"I'll call you Eun Ji?" Joy asked.

No teacher before or ever since called me by that name.

"You can say whatever you want—if you reckon with it." Joy asked me to be relentlessly forgiving and magnanimous toward all conditions of human life, and equally toward those of my own. She encouraged me to look closely, and said poetry would teach me how to pay attention and show me how to care. I must choose love over any other thing. Then, the world would open up for me. "Do you see now?" she asked me. "That's why a poem is more than just words—it's why poets have everything."

15

Hello?

Now that the heat's gone (*hot weather*), fall has shown its face. (*Early mornings*) like today or during nights, it gets pretty chilly.

Even if we keep calling each other, it's not the same as seeing you. It's unsatisfying. Mommy misses Eun Ji, too. (*Probably*) the amount Mommy misses Eun Ji is 10 *times* the amount Eun Ji misses Mommy. For now, it's better than before (since you guys are adults now). Before, I was nearly diagnosed with (*mental depression*) from how much I missed my babies. That's all in the past! (*Time*) felt longer, longer than usual. Now I said it's in the (*past*), but yesterday I went to a (*mission*), a sacred place called "Hauhyeon Catholic Church" where I saw mass, and all these thoughts filled me.

The time we'd gone *camping*, the time I'd lost you inside *Macy's*, the time a mosquito bit your face and you looked like a monster, the time we went to the two-story bathhouse (and blew bubbles), *remember*? How about the time in Gilroy, when you wouldn't budge from in front of the shop when I refused to buy clothes for you until (*finally*) I did? Traveling to and from *Davis* when you guys lived there and Mommy's spilled tears following her. At the time, when I stopped by *Sacramento* church, my heart must've been hurting because I was saddened and cried so many times. Seems like yesterday, but those things already happened four years ago. When Mommy sees mass now—

I don't cry anymore. A long time ago, living was burdensome. For reasons from a long time ago, I had spilled tears while seeing mass. Now I'm seeing mass with an earnest (*acuteness*) but joyous heart. Maybe in this letter Mommy wants to talk about (*peace*).

I'm happy that *John* looks well and Eun Ji seems more at ease than (*before*). Mommy and your dad get along better than before, we have nothing to (*envy*) in our lives. I think the work Mommy can do is pray all she can, give to society, and do what God likes me to do. Of course, when I go back to America, I'll have to work hard. I have to send my Eun Ji to graduate school and John needs to go to graduate school, too. Mommy has to earn as much money as possible. And Eun Ji, let go of the past and focus on yourself. Neither (*happiness*) nor sadness are ever done with us. They are always passing by. Have peace in your heart, love yourself, and comfort yourself. "You're doing so well, Eun Ji. Stay strong!" Just like this. You know?

Eun Ji! Eat your rice. Drink less. Sleep well. Be happy. Bye. *Good Luck*!

Love Mom
May 10, 2010

안녕? 이제 더위 (Hot 한 weather)가 가고
가을이 왔나보다. 이른 아침 (early morning) 이나
저녁으로는 꽤 쌀쌀 하구나.
자주 통화는 하지만 볼 수가 없으니 안타깝구
나. 엄마도 우리 은지가 많이 보고 싶단다.
아마도 (probably) 엄마가 은지 보고 싶은 마음이
은지가 엄마 보고 싶은것의 10 Times 는 되지 싶다.
지금은 많이 좋아졌지만 (너희들이 어른이 되어서)
전에는 우리 새끼들 보고 싶어서 우울증 (mental
depression)에 걸릴 뻔 한 적도 있었어.
다 지난 이야기이지! 참 긴긴 세월 (time) 이었
어. 이젠 그야말로 과거 (past)가 됐지만,
어저께는 성지 (mission) 에 갔었단다
'하우현' 이라는 성당인데 미사보고 하면서 많은
생각이 스치더구나. 옛날에 Camping 갔었던일,
은지를 Macy's 에서 잃어 버렸던 일, 벽이
서에서 은지 얼굴 러물 됐던일, 둘이 같이 이층
목욕탕에서 목욕 (거품배스) 하던일, remember?
길로이 가서 은지가 못 안사 준다고 가게 앞에
서서 꼼짝도 안해서 결국 (finally) 사줬던
Davis 에 너네끼리 살때 엄마가 돌아가며
눈물 쏟았던일, 그때는 Sacramento 성당만
가면 어찌나 가슴 아프고 슬프던지 정말 미사보며
많이 울었단다. 엊그제 같은데 벌써 4년전 일
이 되어 버렸단다. 이제 엄마는 미사보며 은지

않는단다. 더 옛날에는 사는게 힘들고 그래서
그때는 그때대로 가끔씩, 미사 볼때 눈물을
흘리곤 했지만 이젠 정말 감절하지만 기쁜
마음으로 미사를 하고 있단다. (acuteness)

이번 편지에는 엄마가 평화 (peace) 라는 말이
하고 싶은가 보다. 〰️ → Rainbow

John 이도 좋아 보이고 은지도 예전 (before)
보다 많이 안정돼 보여서 너무 좋구나.

엄마도 아빠하고 그 어느때보다 사이좋게 잘
지내고 있고, 세상에 부러울것 (envy) 이 없다.
엄마가 할 수 있는 일은 기도 열심히 하고 사회에
봉사 하면서 하느님이 예뻐 하시는 일을 하는거라는
생각이 든다. 모든 며칠에 돌아가면 열심히 일을
해야겠지. 우리 은지 대학원도 보내야 하고
창현이도 대학원 가야 하니까 엄마가 열심히
돈 벌어야 하거든, 은지도 이제는 지나간 일은
털어 버리고 너만 생각 하도록 해, 사랑 사는일은
늘 지나가는거야. 절대 행복 (happyness)도 불행
도 멈춰 있지는 않아. 그렇게 항상 흐르는거야.
언제나 마음을 편하게 하고 자기 스스로 사랑하며
잘 다독이고 사는거야. "정말 잘하고 있어, 은지야
힘내!" 이렇게 말이야. 알지?

은지! 밥🍔 잘 먹고 🍺 술은 덜 먹고 잠은
잘자고 ᶻᶻ 그렇게 잘지내. 안녕🍀

Love mom — 💗∞   Good Luck!

16

In New York City, two years later, I ran to my first poetry workshop at my graduate program. In a narrow room with high plaster ceilings, eight of us strangers pushed four tables together in the center. The ceiling had handprints on it, but no one knew how they got there. Somebody said the building used to be an insane asylum. "You ever wonder why you can't leave?" he whispered. "The halls and stairs circle you back to where you started." There was a white colonial window, haunted by the morning sun, overlooking the lawn. I loved going to school, reading and writing poetry. I was fortunate to have an internship at Union Square and rented a room on 148th, an apartment I shared with a therapist and a neuroscientist. Some nights I was so tired that I drank the faucet water to get rid of hunger pains and go to bed early. My father once said, about his military training: it is human nature to choose sleep over food amid exhaustion and hunger.

A year after I had graduated in Irvine, and seven years after they had left the country, my parents moved back to California. I was packing to leave for New York City when my mother told me over the phone: "We're finally coming back since your brother has stopped talking to us." My father was afraid of losing his children. While my mother knew that I would be fine, my brother could not wait for them anymore. The day my brother called him, my father put in his notice.

When she said this, I set down my things. "Is that all?"

She said, "Your brother told your dad that he doesn't have parents."

"That's all he said?" I asked her.

"What do you mean, 'that's all?'" she said. "The first contract was three years. The second was two years. The third was another two. Your dad has done *enough* for us. He's had to work every day and stay out drinking because of his boss. If he stays any longer, he'll get liver failure like everybody else."

I was not unaware of my father's work, not in the way she feared, yet I resented his sacrifice. My brother later revealed: he was the one who had encouraged our father to take the job in Korea. He promised our father he would oversee me. My brother was never angry about the job until they asked for more time. It was our parents who, terrified to leave that job, did not come back for us. My brother would say, "I won't ever be like them."

I cleared my throat. "What about your sister? Your brothers?"

"I know. How can I leave them again?" she said. "Will you come and see me? I'm so proud that you're going to school again. Remember when you couldn't talk? Or read a book or tell time?"

My father's company did not cover graduate school costs. I had taken out a hundred-thousand-dollar loan to go to school and live simply to read and write poetry. Now, as they moved to their house in Fremont, I was moving across the country. I would not join them. When my mother asked me if I was happy to have her back anyway, I was not sure whether I should tell her I *was* happy, and then, whether it would be true. Not willing to take time off from school, I lingered on the phone with her, saying nothing as my mother went on and on. She could have been in a prison, the way she went on in the dark.

~

I looked up at the handprints on the ceiling. The others discussed our famous professor. Few were lucky enough to see him walking around the West Village. I could not say that I had heard of him or read his poems. The professor strolled in with a doughnut and took the chair at the end of the table. He was statuesque with sleek white hair and wore a cashmere scarf. He stared at his free hand as though it might have a glass of water. "I'm late because I wanted a doughnut." He then took another bite and surveyed the room. "Tell me what you did before you wrote poetry."

Law school was brought up as well as a family business. One person talked about his parents who read poetry and kept many books in his home. He was always going to write poetry. I had never once seen my mother read a book in English.

The doughnut left a wreath of crumbles around the professor's mouth. He wiped off his mouth and hands with a napkin. When he posed the question to me, I replied, "Nothing."

"Except for you," he said to me, "everybody else has made a grave mistake."

The room laughed, but the professor gave us a serious look.

"If you have something better to be doing than poetry, which means almost *anything* else, that is the thing you should be doing right now," he said to the class. Then, he turned to me. "There's nowhere else you could be?"

"No," I said to him. "Nowhere."

"You made the right choice. Poetry is better than *nothing*," he said to me. "But you have nothing to fall back on." He was careful not to ask any more questions. He must have sensed I was embarrassed to speak in front of the others, who were confident and sharp.

The professor took out the napkin and let it open in his hand. "I'm going to be honest with all of you."

The room looked at each other.

The professor said to the class, "If you have something else, and you can *do* something else, then don't let it go. Most of you will go back to doing that thing."

The professor eyed each of us with suspicion. "Now let's dig into your poems."

~

Most poems I typed quickly in my room on 148th. I read them aloud to hear the words until they lost all reason, and what remained was an urge. Like when I had learned of Kumiko's death in Irvine, I had locked myself in the bathroom, convinced somebody was coming to kill me. What was real was my urge to hide, but nothing else—the shadow-knife, the white sheet. This urge let me write as if my words were final. A harmless day or two without sleep showed as sickness over months. My therapist roommate also managed an Italian restaurant across the street. On occasion, when I stumbled up to the bar, she placed in front of me penne in red and yellow tomato sauce. She stood watching as I put a forkful into my mouth before she traipsed off to another table. After licking my plate, I rushed out the door. I was in the habit of making others worry.

~

For our second poetry workshop, our professor was an Irish poet and translator called Noah. He had a white beard and spoke to us kindly. He was different from the other professors. Noah listened to our poems. While we stared at the floor with regret, he read our poems as if they were complete, regarding their truth and significance better than we ourselves could recognize.

Noah asked the class to translate a poem from any language into English. But I had not translated a poem before. Using a dictionary, I translated a poem written by a Korean poet, who was my mother's high school friend from her journalism club in Daejeon.

Noah ended the day insisting that, whether or not we knew a language, we ought to translate because it serves our poetry. Noah seemed to address me directly: "If you want to be a good poet, then write poetry. If you want to be a great poet, then translate."

He did not offer more than these words.

That same day, I walked into the graduate program office and added a second degree in translation. I inquired to add a third degree but was warned against the workload. At the hall across the lawn, separate from the graduate office, I signed up for one-on-one tutoring twice a week. Normally a service for undergraduates, nobody there advised me against it. I sorted my degree requirements and bought a Korean dictionary.

For my internship, I took work home with me. For school, I went to workshops and tutoring, read on the train, and wrote in the evenings. I counted my cigarettes, turned on a heating pad, and lay down in bed with a bottle of wine that had been left behind in one of the workshops. There was a bodega open across the street where I picked up cans of soup and a lighter. In the morning, the therapist had brought me water and left it outside my locked door. Seeing the water glass, I thought that I must have kept her up all night.

The next semester, I would add the only translation seminar offered—one that would stay with me long after it ended. In the seminar, we would translate ancient poets who retreated into the mountains with nothing and descended after years with answers.

~

Noah read my poem. "These lines," he said. "'For a month I tried to think of what to say. / How many times you've swept a kitchen knife / across your neckline and said, *This is how / you end a marriage.* How many more wicks you light / for God. I could tell by your eyes you've never seen him. What do you call the feeling / of abandon and caution and relief that keeps me / tethered to you?'" Noah paused. "What a wonderful thing to put to words."

"I don't know—"

"You don't know what the poem can do. Be gentle. Even if you feel disappointed. There's nothing to do but leave it alone." You were lucky if Noah, by virtue of admiring your poem, protected it from your own harmful ways.

I cupped my mouth. "How can I be a good poet? I don't even know how to be a good person."

He said sternly, "All you have to be is ready."

~

Our famous professor held his office hours at a diner in the West Village. We met one last time after he had read the poems I had written all semester. He looped a dark wool scarf around his thin neck. He ordered coffee and I asked for hot chocolate. "For all the things you won't say in class, your poems are fairly loud." He leaned back in his booth and asked me, "Do you believe in God?"

"I don't know," I said. "I grew up in a Catholic church."

"Your poems still have God in them," he said.

"How do you not talk about it?"

"What if God isn't real?" he said. "We have to make peace with that."

"But there's design. The world has design."

"It doesn't prove God exists." The professor put a shiny card on the table to pay for his coffee and my hot chocolate. "Do we need God to make meaning?"

Whatever he had wanted to say, he then stopped trying to get it across to me. Any thinking could not do away with the problem of overthinking. We sat in silence for a while.

"I'm just saying, if God didn't exist," he said, "would it be so terrible?"

"If we didn't get to wonder about it, maybe it would be."

We finished our drinks, and I followed him out.

"If I could go back, I don't even know if I'd choose poetry," he said. "You are working way too hard, Angela. It's only poetry. I am not the happiest person in the world."

Before we parted ways, he advised me to slow down and find an answer for myself. It was possible that the answer I looked for was hidden somewhere other than in my poems. He himself had taken up other things to do such as walking and going into the kitchen to prepare himself a meal. Only when I left him could I hear his warning. Doing things other than writing helped him to see poetry for what it was and to understand life for what it should have been for him.

~

That night, looking out the window of my room on 148th, I ignored my desk and watched the storefronts and houses regurgitate objects through their doorways. They spewed refrigerators, trees with string lights, trash bags impaled by coat hangers, lovely inflatable pools, children racing onto the sidewalks, trays of steamed dumplings, a quartet of oboes and strings, a rack of cocktail dresses, and big voices that carried over the cars and crowds and construction.

I sat down against the foot of my bed. I was trying to muster up courage for something I was not yet prepared to do. When I closed my eyes, Mieko's wings brushed against my cheek. My mother called but I did not pick up the phone, choosing instead to let it ring. At midnight, an ambulance charged down the road. Red flags waved above my room, then disappeared. The horn blared long and hard.

Then I dialed a number I had never called before.

"Where are you?" a male voice asked.

"Home," I said.

"How long have you been there?"

The voice sounded about my age.

I said, "It's my birthday."

"I'm glad you called," he said.

"The suicide hotline?"

"Mm-hmm," he said.

I wiped my face and noticed dark drops on my shirt from tears. Each time I breathed I had trouble, but I did not understand why it was happening now.

"Is everything all right?" he asked.

"Can you tell me what you tell people on the phone?"

"Of course," he said. "I can do that."

"Okay, I'm listening."

"Well, first, I ask where they are because I want to make sure they're not in any danger," he said, thoughtful not to include me in his explanation. "I also want to know what's happening around them. If they can get to a better place, that makes a difference. Once they're in a safe place, I ask about what's exactly hurting them. If they know the problem, they can always work on a plan."

I looked at my surroundings. I had dragged a blanket to cover my legs.

I asked him, "What's your name?"

"Ben," he said.

Ben must have been in his twenties and trained hard because he never interrupted. He was slow-speaking, and his voice was pacifying. I wondered what he looked like in person.

"Have you ever been in love?" I asked.

"Of course," he said. "Have you?"

"I think so—I hope so."

"Do you have any plans today?"

"I did have plans," I said.

"How about tomorrow?" he asked.

"I want to go home," I said. "Do you think I can—go?"

Our famous professor had given his students a copy of his new book. In its pages, I would find a God, and it would not bother me. After leaving the program, I would learn of his death, but it was then that he would teach me an enormous lesson. He was not just a great poet, but a person who had lived in a way that others saw in him a greatness, and in themselves, the belief that such greatness can exist.

"I don't know how to get rid of the urge to take my life," I said to Ben. "I had never thought about it seriously before. But there must be a difference between *having* a life and *being* a life. The first one, I can let go. The second, I can't ever let go—no matter what. Maybe that's the good news. Whether or not I keep living, I am life."

Ben's voice reached for me. He begged me not to hang up the phone.

17

Hello?

It's been a while since I've written to my beloved daughter. I am thankful that you're busy passing the time. Honestly, writing letters is difficult for me, but because of Eun Ji, it feels like I can practice writing again. All of a sudden, it came to mind that Eun Ji must enjoy seeing Mommy's letters, but Eun Ji also asks for the letters to give Mommy an opportunity to write. If so, Mommy is, again, thankful for that!

(*Last weekend*), your dad, Daejeon Auntie, and I went to watch the (*lotus*) flowers bloom. It's a place called Buyeo, 1 hour and 30 minutes even from Daejeon, and there was a wide-open space, about 360,000 sq. feet, bursting full of lotus flowers. Later, I'll show you a photo. It was elegant and cool. Long time ago, during the Baekje Kingdom, it was the *king's* (*garden*). Auntie wanted to see it badly, but her husband doesn't take trips, so we went together. For lunch, we ate at a restaurant where they use the lotus flowers to wrap the rice. On Sunday, I met with friends and had fun playing. Mommy's playing so well that she feels sorry to her babies, you know?

But how's the (*weather*) over there? Over here, it's hot. It's excruciatingly hot. Every day it goes over 100 degrees Fahrenheit. And do you know? That *sticky* and *wet* feeling. That's why Mommy *cut* her hair. Short. People said I look young. Huhuhu, then that's good!

Yesterday, I liked hearing Eun Ji's voice over the phone. Now you are calmer (*stability or stabilization*). You feel relaxed (*keep equilibrium*, or *calm*). It's truly a relief. Try not to overthink. Of course, you don't have the most time, but *take your time in doing your work*. Everything you think is difficult becomes that much more difficult, doesn't it? Really, Eun Ji has raised herself (*admirably*). Mommy is thankful to God first and *thankful* to Eun Ji. (*Please*) take care of your body, eat your rice, you must. You know, right? I'll write again. *Bye bye.*

– The world is a fun place. We are not born
  to win or lose against others. I am here to
  be happy for myself.

– An elephant does not think its trunk is
  heavy. If that is one's (*destiny, fate*) and

(*responsibility*), there is no weight, but
rather, importance.

– What we see changes according to what we
look for.

– God (*disciplines*, *trains*) humans by using
time, not by cracking (*a switch*).

– In any suffering, happiness is crouched
inside. We just don't know where good and
bad reside.

– If you love yourself, everything rolls along
as it should. If you want to *accomplish*
something, truly love yourself.

– Because faces are like books, people will
read me on my face. (Continuously keep
a good heart, guarding a *peaceful* life, and
your expressions will read well.)

The above words I've jotted down from a book I'm reading
called *Good Thoughts*. If you read and keep them in mind,
they'll be helpful. *I Love You, Eun Ji and miss you.*

August 10, 2010

안녕? 사랑하는 우리 딸에게 오랫만에 편지를 쓴다.
바쁘게 잘지내고 있다니 정말 고마운 일이구나.
사실 편지 쓰는게 참 어려운데 은지 덕분에 엄마가 글쓰기
연습을 하는것 같다. 갑자기, 은지가 엄마 편지 보는 재미도
있지만 엄마한테 글을 쓱 가르쳐 주려고 그러는게 아닌가
생각이 들었다. 그렇다면 그 또한 고마운 일이지!
지난 주말 (last weekend)에는 아빠하고 대전이모 하고
같이 연꽃 (Lotus) 구경하러 갔었어.
부여라는 곳인데 대전에서도 1시간 30 분 이나 걸리는 곳이 있구,
360000 sq feet 이나 되는 넓은곳에 온통 연꽃 특성이 있어.
나중에 사진 보여 줄게. 예쁘고 멋있고 그랬어.
옛날 우리나라 백제 4대 왕의 정원 (garden) 이었대.
이모가 많이 가보고 싶어 했는데 이모부가 어디 안다니시니까
우리랑 간거지. 그 연꽃 앞에 서서 방을 해주는데 가서
점심도 먹고 일요일엔 친구들 만나서 놀고 재미있게 잘 지냈단다.
엄마 너무 세끼를 한테 미안 할만큼 잘 놀고 있지? ㅎㅎ
그런데 그곳 날씨 (weather)는 어떠니?
여긴 정말 덥단다. 정말 더워, 매일 100°F 가 넘는것 같애.
그리고 알지? sticky 하고 wet 한 느낌 말이야.
그래서 엄마 머리 cut 했단다. 짧게.
사람들이 젊어 보인대. ㅎㅎㅎ 그러면 됐지!
어저께 전화통에 은지 목소리 들으니 좋더라.
이젠 많이 안정되고 (stability or stabilization) 안본래 있게
느껴졌단다. 정말 다행이야.   • keep equilibri
근데 너무 바쁘게 생각 하지마. 몸도   • 아니면 calm
시간이 아주 많은건 아니지만
take your time in doing your work.
뭐든 너무 힘들게 생각 하면 그만큼 힘들어 지는거니까. 그지?
정말 은지가 기특하게 (admirable) 잘 자라 주었어.
엄마는 우선 하느님께 감사하고 우리은지에게 thank 한다.
부디 (please) 몸조심 하고 밥 잘먹고 그래야 해. 알지?
또 쓸께. bye bye   2010. 08. 10

＊ 세상은 재미 있는 곳이다.
우리는 남들한테 이기거나 지려고 태어난것이 아니라
내 몫 만큼 즐겁게 살려고 운명이다.

＊ 그끼너는 자기르는 무겁게 여기지 않는다.
그게 자신의 운명 이고 책임 이라면
무거움기 있고 destiny   responsibility
fate
즐거할 뿐이다.

＊ 우리가 보는것은
우리가 찾는것에 따라 달라진다.

＊ 신은 한가르가 아닌 시간으로 인간을 단련시킨다.
a switch   training
discipline.
＊ 어떤 불행속에도 행복이 없으려고 있다.
어디에 좋은 일이, 어디에 나쁜일이 있는지 우리가
모를 뿐이다.

＊ 자신을 사랑하면 모든것이 제대로 흘러간다.
무언가를 성취 하고 싶다면 진실로 자신을 사랑하라.
accomplishment

＊ 얼굴은 책과 같아서 사랑들은 내 얼굴에서 나를 읽는다.
(늘 좋은 마음으로 평화 (peace) 를 지키며 살면
얼굴 표정도 좋아 진다)

〰 위에 써 놓은 말들은 엄마가 읽는 '좋은 생각'
이라는 책에 나온 것 들이간다.
잘 새겨서 읽으면 도움이 될거야.

" I Love You, Eun Ji "

and MISS You.

18

After my father resigned from the company, they sold their house in California and put their savings into a small motel in Washington. When I entered their lobby, my parents were offering their guests tea. My mother spoke some English and used gestures to ask her guests if they would like to meet her daughter. My father understood that Americans were serious about privacy. He never knocked on their doors without calling first. My mother knocked anyway, insisting that nothing was as urgent as fresh doughnuts in the lobby. Though her guests loved her, she saved the big and tasty doughnuts for those who worked in the laundry room, where she told funny stories of her years at the dry cleaners. She acted out herself sobbing in the bathroom, rubbing her fists over her eyes, boohooing, as they chortled between bites. "Your lives will get better," she said, perched on a washing machine. "Look at me. Look." Her guests endured the sight of a grander hotel across the street, but the motel was perfect for families.

After graduate school, nine years after my parents had left the country, I moved from New York City to live with them, reunited at last in their apartment on an island near Seattle. The island had twisted brambles of blackberries as dark as our eyes, toy boats washed ashore by real boats crossing Lake Washington, and bright new asphalt over the roads. On weekdays, I taught poetry at a local writing center. My students, older than me, eyed me with distrust. By our last class, they embraced me to disburden me of their doubts. With teaching, it took months to unpack—a task to get through even a single box. I sorted folders one night when my mother called me into the kitchen, where she was cooking mackerel for my father.

My father complained to my mother so that I could hear him, "You never make me fish because you say it'll stink up the apartment. But you make fish for your *daughter*."

"It's hard to cook for only two people," she said cheerfully. "Now that it's the three of us together, we can eat something delicious. Nine years, can you believe it?"

"I can have all the fish I want!" my father roared.

I asked my mother in English, "Deep-fried?"

"No, the one in the pan." She said in English, "Pan-fried."

My father watched the construction across the street.

My mother suggested remodeling the motel. Then she said to me, "You haven't changed at all. But your Korean is better—"

"I don't like fish," I said.

"You don't like fish?" she asked.

"I haven't liked fish for years."

"Oh." My mother took the pan off. "Is that true?"

My father became quiet as he set the table.

"We can go out to eat," my mother offered.

My father said to her evenly, "We can eat alone."

She said to me, "Don't think too hard about it—"

"I'm not hungry," I said.

"But it tastes so good," she said to me. "I've been standing on my feet all day for work, and I come home to cook so we can eat together. Don't you feel sorry for me?"

My father asked me, "What are you going to do for work?"

His question surprised me. "I'm working—"

"No, you're not." My mother sat herself at the table. "You're teaching poetry."

My father paused. "You're not a complete person if you don't work." He believed all paths lead to work. There is work that each of us must do at every point in our lives. Work can change but working cannot. Every pleasure seeks to achieve what feeling is achieved by working. "Work gives purpose, it takes away suffering," he said. "Our work is the motel—what's yours?"

I was confused about how to find what they would accept as meaningful work. "Work," he called it, as if it were the only word to trust with our lives.

Having a motel suited them. The motel was an endless list of tasks. They could have retired but my parents struggled between two halves of the past and the future, as if the former might catch up to take revenge upon them. While they worked at the motel, fixing pipes and flooded toilets, I forsook my afternoons at the writing center. My mother asked, "Why do you write poems? You should do work that gives you confidence and a tall straight back. How can you rely on poetry when you can't rely on yourself?"

My mother had lost her desire to cook and wanted to eat out at a restaurant. She turned off the lights, room to room, in the apartment. From the dark hallway, she asked me, "Do you know what happens when you don't work for many years? Your children look down on you."

Seeing one another seemed unnecessary when you lived together.

~

I was still unpacking in the morning when I found a clear plastic box. Smaller than a shoebox, it was stuffed with tissue paper. Shaking the box, I heard a thud inside. At the bottom was a bundle of mail. It was the letters my mother had posted from Korea. I thought I had thrown them out years ago. Maybe I had intended to reread them one day. I had not known Korean then the way I could read it now. Before I was able to finish a letter, I returned it to its envelope, and the envelope to its box. I counted the letters. There were forty-nine.

What I had meant to say in the kitchen was that I had loved fish since I was little—white bite, crispy skin. I had been waiting for it so long that the picture of soft flesh decomposed and left bones for a fossil. When I had argued in the kitchen, I was arguing about what was lost to me. Like how I could not read the letters because of the old water stains that had spread ink across the bottom of the page. The problem was not the damage but the cause. I recognized the tears my younger self had wept while touching the shapes on the paper.

~

It drizzled lightly as I waited on the steps of the Seattle Asian Art Museum. I had brought with me my mother's letters in a large envelope, which I covered with my coat as one might shield a child in the rain. From the direction of the road, I heard a rumbling noise. A car swept into the lot and parked in front of me.

I had shipped my thesis to my committee before graduation. My poems had been accepted by my adviser and a professor in my department, but my poetry translations were read by someone I had never met. The school must have hired a Korean translator to read my work. His name was Dae Hee. Beyond his name, I knew nothing about him.

Dae Hee had responded to my email the night before, which I sent him after arriving to this city. To my surprise, he had been living in Seattle for years. Dae Hee had agreed to meet in person at the museum. When I had told him about my mother's letters, he was happy to look at them.

A figure appeared out of the driver's side.

When she scuffled toward me in a long pullover, her face framed by short black hair with few grays and thick glasses— over her shoulder, a canvas bag of Korean magazines—I realized I had made a mistake. The name I had read was Dae Hee. There had been a misprint, or I had misread her name. It should have read Da Hee.

"Da Hee," she said, introducing herself. She embraced me. "Think of all the places you could've gone. But you've landed on my doorstep in Seattle." She laughed and pulled out an umbrella. "You'll get soaked. Follow me."

Da Hee led me past the museum lot and between arching oaks into a fifty-acre park. We crossed a hidden trail of thorny shrubs. She warned me about the sharp leaves of blueberry bushes. Though she came to the height of my shoulders, Da Hee kept her arm high so I could walk under her umbrella. "Isn't it special," she said, "to meet like this?"

We approached a circular red brick tower, and Da Hee guided me around the vine-covered walls to a small passage-way. She told me that it was a water tower, or at least that was what she had heard. From the top, she could point me toward the dahlia gardens and the koi ponds. She squeezed my hand. "It's one of my favorite places," she said.

Entering the tower, she pointed to the 107 steps winding up toward the lookout. I knew it had stopped raining because I could no longer hear the raindrops outside the doorway. Adjusting my grip on the handrail, I started the long climb behind her. Only the sounds of our footsteps surrounded us.

"I feel like I'm getting old," Da Hee said at the top. She giggled. We gathered our things and sat on a stone bench in front of a carved-out square lookout to the green fields that would not be out of place in a fond recollection of a dream.

I gave her the large envelope. Da Hee fanned the letters out on her lap. She read them quietly. Da Hee glanced up, then back down. "Are there more?" she asked me.

"It's all there was in the box," I said. "Just the forty-nine."

"Forty-nine?" Da Hee fixed her glasses on her nose. She paused at the letter where my mother had drawn her permed hair. Da Hee flipped through pages covered with the bright-colored ink of glitter pens that my mother had picked out at the stationery store.

"I've looked at them," I said.

"But have you read them recently?" she asked.

I did not want to read them alone because I had made them dead. I made them dead so that I could live without them. "No," I said.

"What if you translated them?" she asked. "You can read them with fresh eyes."

"Translate them?"

She said, "Of course, you're a translator!"

The umbrella she had leaned against our bench had a little pool around it. She returned the letters to the large envelope and handed the envelope to me. Da Hee adored adventure. Fear was temporary to her, a hesitation to overcome. "Your mother is lucky to have you," she said. "You are a good daughter."

I warned her that she might be mistaken, and she said it was impossible. She cautioned me to keep my mother's letters in good condition.

"How exciting for you—there's something else," Da Hee exclaimed. "You have forty-nine letters." She collected her things and led me down the stairs and outside the tower. "When you die, your soul wanders the earth for answers before the afterlife." Da Hee checked for rain before she put her umbrella in her canvas bag. "This transition between life and death takes forty-nine days," she said to me. "It means this is your work."

I bowed to her in the parking lot and waited for her car to turn onto the street before I raised my head again and began my walk home.

~

Toward the end of summer, I headed to an artists' residency in New Hampshire where the leaves changed to yellow and red across 450 acres of woods. My cabin was furnished with a dusty 1988 Steinway piano and a rocking chair. On a table by the window, I translated my mother's letters. I re-lived the presence of that oak tree in the backyard in Davis. The distance from the house to the grass park across the road. The hallways of the school widening into terminals of airports. My morning visits to the tiny grave at the fence where I walked myself in circles. My voice neither trembled to make the round sounds of the Korean, as if I were gently stirring a saucepan, nor did I wonder in my heart if I could recognize them.

I looked up at the vivid foliage of the woods, the rapidly darkening forest. In the distance, the library lights would come on, as if a kerosene lamp held in the air—a sign that others were nearby. While my mother liked cleanliness, I was satisfied to have my presence linger. Whereas she erased any traces of herself, wiping the surfaces clean, I left myself behind. My cabin smelled of coffee and cigarettes. It was disarranged with notecards, papers, boards, and a dictionary. There were fingerprints over the piano keys. The rocking chair, positioned askew.

I walked over a footpath to find myself upon an open meadow. Then, turning, I went to my cabin, shaking with courage the whole way. As the door closed behind me, I flooded with tears unlike ever before, not even during childhood. I let myself cry for no reason through the night, and for those many nights long ago.

~

My mother was born at 8 o'clock on a May morning in Daejeon. Pale and golden and edible, a soybean—not five pounds—she was merciful to her mother Jun. Lee had worried about Jun's weak body. However, his daughter knew this and arrived small to fit modestly into their lives, keep them together. But she could not bear a second without Jun. She wailed, hurting her throat. Using a large square cloth, Jun had no choice but to tie her daughter to her belly and take her along when using the bathroom. Lee waited for them outside. Jun said, facing her daughter, that she must not cry so uncontrollably. There's a lot to be happy about, my daughter. Can't you see it with your eyes freshly placed by God? There is nothing to fear. No revenge, only us.

~

My last week in New Hampshire, I read to a group in a private room in the library. There were paintings, gold-leafed books, and chandeliers. At the podium, I read two translations of her letters. I read as my mother writing to her daughter. I paused where she would have paused. I chuckled where she must have chuckled. To be a translator is to speak in your mother's voice.

When I finished, I stared out into the room and through the back window toward the footpath leading into the forest. The porch light of my cabin had finally gone out.

After the reading, I searched for a glass of water in the main building. One of the other residents caught up to me. The old man cracked open a beer and followed me to the porch. "You left so quickly," he said to me. "You're going back to work tonight?"

"Yeah, I think so," I said.

"Can I ask you something?" he said. "Why didn't your dad go by himself?"

"My mother had family in Korea. She wanted to go—"

He nodded. "Why didn't they make you come with them?"

"I told them I'd stay here——"

"You can't choose at that age," he said. "Anybody hearing your letters would ask you these things."

"Yes, they might. They might wonder," I said.

"But if your dad didn't take the job? Did he have a good job here?"

"He did," I said. "He'd also never get a job like that if he stayed."

"Their reasons for going, I don't know," he said. "They abandoned you." He tilted his can back. He meant that he would never have considered it. "I got two daughters."

"Sure," I said. "It bothers you——"

"I can't even write about my parents," he said. "They're still alive."

"You know my grandmothers," I said, and pointed at my nose, a habit I had picked up when I lived in Japan. "I'm an accumulation of their lives. Whatever I say or do now can give relief to the past—and to them. I don't believe they're ever gone."

"That's interesting," he said. "I still wouldn't do it."

"My parents didn't give me happiness," I said. "But they set me free. They gave me freedom."

The old man laughed and tossed his can, then headed off the porch toward his cabin. He stopped and spun around to ask me, "Do you think my daughters would miss me? Do you think they'd wait for me—like you waited for them?"

19

My beloved daughter!

You're doing well, aren't you? What's the weather like where my Eun Ji lives? Korea is scorching. Because it's sticky, and because it rains a lot, I'm irritated. Days like these keep coming. Eun Ji studies and suffers while Mommy plays and complains about hot weather . . . I'm sorry. But I can't study in your place, you know.

It's been a week since I wrote you a letter, but I don't know if you read it. Your dad finally bought a camera. I repeatedly told him to use Eun Ji's *old one*, but he kept whining (?) so he *ordered* a new one off the Internet. It's an *Olympus* and I don't think it's very good. If he was going to buy one, he should've bought a better one *anyway*, like your (*you*) new one with the *lens* sticking out the front. But he must have bought a cheap one. After he got it, he was whining again. Anyway, he wants to go play somewhere this *weekend*. Maybe he wants to take photographs. That's why we're going to Dae Doon Mountain to ride a cable car. There's supposedly a *hot spring*. Sounds nice, doesn't it? I know, Mommy likes taking trips. (*Fortunately*), these days, your dad wants to go somewhere by the time it's Saturday or Sunday, so I'm happy.

If Eun Ji hears this, she might feel burdened, but Mommy and Daddy have big (*expectations*) of you. *We know we must not expect too much of you.* Even so, just thinking about it makes me happy. (*Especially*) because Mommy didn't study as hard as she could, and I regretted it a lot. There were several reasons. But my whole life, I regretted it.

I would like my Eun Ji to try your best. It becomes the foundation (*base*) for your (*whole life*). The more (*all the more*) you'll have your own (*yourself*) self-esteem, and down the road, Eun Ji will become a (*good example*) to your children. You know this, right? Yes, but don't tire yourself. (Because you can quit whenever you want.) But think of it as a challenge to your own courage, and for now, do all that you can. I would like you to do that. *Fighting*!!!

Mommy and your dad, too. When we think of going back to America, our hearts get busy. We get scared. But we are spending our lives (*time?*) with cheerful hearts. Now there are not many months left! When we go back, we'll live seeing our babies often. Even the thought makes me happy. Mommy will pick up some kind of work, so it seems she will live a more fulfilling life, too. Mommy wants to work. Your dad wants to rest. "Mommy wants to work." Work to make money. Work that contributes to the world. Work that helps others. Work which gives a (*vivid*) feeling that everything is alive. I'm saying that Mommy also wants to show you that she is (*capable, able*). Mommy wants to show herself and show your dad and you guys. (Hey, I couldn't draw it very good. It's a fist with a thumbs up . . .)

My Eun Ji! I wish you'll always take care of your health and sleep well at night. You know Mommy misses you, right? I love you. My Eun Ji.

August 17, 2010

사랑하는 우리딸! 잘 지내고 있지? ①

우리은지가 사는곳은 날씨가 어떤가? 한국은 너무 덥다.
게다가 끈끈하고 비가 많이 와서 짜증나는 날 들이
계속되고 있단다.
은지는 공부 하느라 고생이 많은데 엄마는 놀기만 하면서
덥다고 투정하다니.... 미안 하구나.
공부는 대신 해 줄 수 있는게 아니니까 말이야.
지난번 편지 인편지 일주일은 지난거 같은데
받았는지 모르겠다.

아빠가 드디어 카메라를 샀단다.
은지것, old one 그냥 쓰라고 그렇게 말했는데
맨날 찡찡 (?) 대더니 인터넷으로 order 해서
받았단다. olympus 건데 별로 안좋은거 같애.
카메라 사는거 잘 알지 않고, Anyway 네꺼 새거 산거
<u>you (내→I)</u>
같이 Lens가 없으로 나쁜거 그런거 말야.
근데 그냥 쓰는거 샀나봐. 또 받아놓고 찡찡 대더라
어쨌든 이번 weekend에 놀러 가자.
사진 찍고 싶나봐. 그래서 대둔산에 케이블카 타러
갈꺼야. Hot spring 도 있나봐.
그래도 덥겠지? 그래 엄마는 여행 다니는거 좋아하거든.
다행히 (fortunate) 요즈음에는 아빠가 토요일 일요일반
모면 어디 가자고 해서 좋단다.

은지가 들으면 부담이 되겠지만, 엄마 아빠는 은지한테
기대 (expectation)가 크단다. We know, we must
not expect too much of you. 그래도 생각만 하면
행복하다.
특히 (specially) 엄마는 나중에 공부를 열심히 안해서
후회가 많단다. 여러가지 이유가 있었지만 정말
많이 후회 하면서 산았거든.

우리은지는 한번 역상히 해보면 좋겠구나.
평생 (whole life)이 멀거는 (Base)이 될거야.
the more (all the more), 네자신 (yourself)
스스로 자랑스러울꺼구, 나중에 은지 자식들 한테도
모범이 (good example) 될거야. 알지?
그래, 그런데 너무 힘들게 하지는 말어라.
(언제든지 그만 둘 수도 있는거니까.)
but, 너 자신와의 싸움이라 생각하고 우선은 최선을
다하면 좋겠구나. fighting !!!

엄마. 아빠는 또 미국에 돌아갈 생각을 하면
마음이 아프단다. 걱정도 되고.
그래도 기쁜 마음으로 세월을 보내고 있다.
                    (Time을)
이제 몇달 안 남았잖아!
돌아가면 우리 새끼들 하고 자주 만나고 살아야지.
생각만 해도 행복하다.
또 엄마도 뭔가 일을 하게 될테니까 훨씬 더
즐겁게 살 수 있을것 같구나.
엄마는 일을 하고 싶고 아빠는 쉬고 싶어하고 그렇다.
"엄마는 일을 하고 싶다"

돈버는 일. 세상에 도움이 되는 일. 남을 도와 주는일
어든지 살아 있다는 느낌이 생생한 일을 하고 싶다.
엄마도 능력 (ability)(Capability 있는거) 이 있다는걸
보여주고 싶단 말이야. 엄마 스스로 한테 또
아빠하고 너희들 한테도. (👍→ 이이 잔뜩 그렸다.
                              주먹쥐고 엄지손가락 올린건데…)

우리은지!
항상 건강에 조심하고 밤에 잠 좀 잘자면 좋겠다.
엄마가 너무 보고 싶어 하는거 알지?
사랑해, 우리은지.
                              8/17/2010

20

On my twenty-seventh birthday, my mother sat in the passenger seat. We drove three hours east from Seattle to the outskirts of Tieton. I had been invited to teach at a week-long poetry retreat in eastern Washington. It was our first trip with just the two of us. Since driving alone daunted me, I had declined the invitation. For years, riding in cars had not bothered me until it did. But my mother had offered to come along if we stopped by the apple orchards on the way in Yakima. While it was still autumn, she had said, rising on her toes in anticipation, she wanted to buy a bushel of apples for my brother and father.

The retreat staff arranged our lodging in cabin 2, directly on the grounds at Wisconsin Street and close to the warehouse where our readings would take place. The cabin was painted green, a private unit that slept two, with a bathroom, kitchen, and queen bed. The staff had left a note on the table about a banquet on Saturday. There was a grocery store nearby in town. We were surrounded by sweeping plains.

I planned for the next morning's class on the table. The retreat director had asked for class descriptions beforehand to print in their schedule. I had assured him it would be a generative workshop. But I did not know yet how best to guide the workshop so that students could write new poems waiting to be written by only them. They say a person has so unique a set of meanings we ought to be incapable of under-standing each other, yet we speak and teach as if by magic.

My mother walked around, then started to clean. She wiped down the table legs with napkins she had nabbed at our last stop on the road. She lifted the table to get the floor underneath the legs, and my papers fell to the floor.

"What am I supposed to do?" she asked me, pulling back the curtains to run a finger along the windowsill. "It's tidy but it's dusty and old." She stopped halfway and said, "You know what? I don't want to clean. I'm getting tired always fixing toilets at the motel."

I picked up my papers. "Really?" I asked her. "Well, are you hungry?"

My mother stared out the window. "We're in the middle of nowhere."

"Sometimes that's nice. Are you bored?"

"I'm starving," she said. "Do you know anybody?"

Setting my papers aside, I explained to her, "Everyone is a part of the retreat. All these cabins are for teachers. If you need anything, just ask somebody."

"I'll tell them I'm your mom. They might think I'm your sister!" She threw her head back and laughed. "But what if I get lost?"

"The town is really small," I said. "It's impossible."

"The post office looks like a museum. Are they normally painted baby blue like that? I've never seen a post office look so cute and small."

"If you wait a little, I can go with you. You want to take pictures, don't you? Do you want to buy something to eat?"

"No, no." She cupped her face. "You finish your work."

"Are you sure?" I asked her. "Where are you going?"

"Don't worry about me," she said. "Wouldn't it be nice if they had a bathhouse? Then we can scrub each other's backs. Your skin doesn't glow as you get older—you need to go to the bathhouse to have glowing skin."

"That's not glowing," I said. "You're just bright red and you have scratches all over your back that don't go away for days—"

"Don't get so upset," she said, and quickly left the cabin.

My mother returned with two burritos wrapped in foil and extra sauces she laid out over a quilt of napkins on the table. "Let's have a picnic." She split the burritos in halves. "Are you done with your lesson plan—?"

"How's it in town?" I interrupted her.

She beamed, "Their one grocery store? It's owned by a Korean woman. I told her I would bring her some apples.

She told me to shut up, in her country voice, you know? She lives here so she has boxes of apples. She loaded six of them in your car. What a strong old woman! She wants to be friends with me."

"Six boxes?" I asked. "How are you going to eat them all?"

"Don't ask such a silly question." Her eyes grew wide. "Your brother and father love apples. We eat apples every day."

"How did you guys load the boxes yourselves?"

"Come with me," she said, standing up. "She has a daughter and I told her I have one too. Let me show you off. Just say hello and pick something out from her store like a stick of gum. She said she'll give it to you for free."

"Why won't you pick out a stick of gum?"

"No," she said. "You have to pick it out—"

Holding up my papers, I asked, "What about this?"

"It's your *birthday*," she said.

I had not figured out a plan for tomorrow. "I don't know—"

"Oh, just do this one thing. This is more important, isn't it?"

~

The next morning, I grumbled out of the cabin without a plan for my workshop. My mother chased after me and bowed to any staff who stopped to say hello. As we walked past the kitchen near the warehouse, my mother grabbed the last banana in the fruit basket before catching up to me again.

She bragged how she fought for it and won against an old man with a mosquito net hat. Our class locations were spread across the buildings. Mine was inside a paper store with a long craft table that seated fifteen, but first I snapped a picture of my mother, who posed in front of the baby-blue post office. "Your workshop," she said. "You've done it a hundred times, haven't you?"

I opened the door for her into the paper store. "No," I said.

She followed me with a folder of extra paper. "Just in case," she said.

The students began to arrive through the door. I added chairs from other parts of the store for the twenty students who had arrived early. Another four wandered in, bringing chairs with them. My mother stood stiff against the book-case wall behind the students, observing them. Her mouth opened and closed; then, finally, she was filled with energy. "Hello, hello," she greeted the students. "Welcome, this is my daughter's class."

The students swiveled their heads between us.

"I have six boxes of apples in the car," my mother announced. "Does anybody want some apples to take home?"

For two hours, my mother shadowed me and the twenty-four students inside the paper store. First during our intro-ductions when she clapped for each student, and then as we worked quietly in our seats.

I wrote about a place called Alki Beach. When I had first crossed the bridge into West Seattle, I could see the city skyline over Puget Sound. I stood on a strip of purple-gray beach sand. A pier house sold hairy mussels and one-hour bike rentals. Copper and metal signs whipped against the wind. Old couples toted bouquets under wooden pergolas. Those singing and strolling on the beach eventually curved around the bend toward the northern arc and out of sight. I wanted to live here by its waters, read its signs, admire the wind as one admires an old friend. The skyscrapers across the water might be a bracelet across my wrist—the Ferris wheel, city stadium, ships in the harbor. I had never known that joy was a practice the way poetry was a practice.

Somebody asked if they could write about love.

The students glanced up from their papers.

"You can write about anything," I said. "Anything you can reckon with."

All this time, my mother waited. Another hour passed, then three had gone by all together. Whenever we met eyes, my mother raised her folder, asking with her gesture if I needed paper. When I looked up at her again, she was already holding a sheet of paper in the air.

~

In the afternoon, I read poems for the retreat in the warehouse. The warehouse was decorated with string lights, cast-iron chandeliers, and haystacks for benches. My mother followed me inside and disappeared. From the stage, I found her in the back, sitting atop one of the haystacks closest to the door where the outside light cast her outline. She was hugging herself, or she was grasping the folder of blank paper to her chest.

After the reading, my mother wiped her eyes. She took the hands of those who had sat with her in the warehouse. The lights inside had come on in preparation for the banquet. Everyone else gathered outside at the fire pit. Those who stared into their notepads entered a private place, but my mother intruded upon them with a long embrace. She confided in them, "My daughter reminds me of my mom. My mom loved poetry. When my mom died, I couldn't even cry."

Leaving her new friends, my mother rushed over to me. Behind her, one of the students gestured that she was in love with my mother. I waved her off and smiled.

"What's wrong?" I asked my mother.

She said, "Did you see the way they look at me?"

"Who?" I asked. "Who did?"

"No, it's not that, Eun Ji." Her eyes searched mine, but my eyes never gave her anything. "Your poems are about Korea, aren't they? Everybody wanted to ask me questions. They were so nice to me. All these people said, 'I'm so happy to meet you, Mrs. Koh.'"

"What did you say?" I was still afraid, falling until her next words. Even if what you fear is not happening, your body and mind cannot tell the difference. "What's wrong?"

"I told them my daughter is a poet," she said, "and I'm her mommy."

When I stepped back from her, she looked hurt. "What else?" I asked and snatched the folder out of her hands. "What else do you know?"

"Eun Ji, I told them about you: You liked poetry because you had a lot of pain in your heart. When you wrote a poem, you were so surprised you felt a little better." She put an imaginary book before us and flipped its pages. "Pretty soon, you asked your poems questions about your life. You're sitting in your room, learning. Right now? You have no idea how long you'll write poetry for—maybe one day you'll say, 'It's not for me anymore!' You don't know what's coming, but I know everything. You were supposed to be a poet. In a previous life, you died with the wish to come back and tell people the truth."

"Stop," I said, exhausted. "Stop talking—"

"How long will you punish me?" she asked.

My mother refused to come back to the cabin until I apologized. But I could not say sorry because of how it might feel to see the pride in her face, as if the way I had grown taller and prouder was a result of her raising me.

~

Seven months later, when my mother had guests from Korea staying at my parents' new house in Bellevue, I recalled our trip. My mother brought out barley tea on a tray into the living room. Her slippers shuffled over the wooden floors. She had purchased white couches and cushions. She coaxed me to show myself to her guests. I stood against the wall and stared at the rug. One guest asked her, "What does your daughter do for work?"

"You mean my only daughter?" my mother said with a grin. "She's buying her first house this year, did you know?"

"Where?" her guest asked. "Where can she live?"

"Alki Beach," my mother said. "Sight unseen."

"On a beach? Sight unseen? How daring like her mother—"

"She's scarier than me," my mother said. "I am fulfilled."

"You'll have to go shopping for the house."

My mother said, "It needs fixing up. But I'm giving her all of my things, like my coffee table. When I die, I don't want her to have to take care of my belongings."

"You're giving it away so you can buy new things," the guest accused her. "Maybe I have some things to give her—"

"Ask your own daughter first. She might get jealous and then you'll be a lonely woman," my mother said, and everyone laughed.

"Won't it be too far away?" her guest asked me, and then turned to my mother. "Well, come on now. The tea is getting cold. What's your daughter's work already?" Days would go by without my thinking of those years we had lived apart until a question like this one reminded me.

I glanced over at my mother who brought the cup to her lips. "You wouldn't understand," she said, and frowned. "My daughter teaches people how to let go."

~

On an early morning in January, when the clouds have lost their muscle, my mother boiled a pot of water with beef, onions, and garlic. She added oval rice cakes and topped it with egg whites and green onions. She poured the white soup into ceramic bowls, stirring each with a ladle as sunlight passed through the window slats, landing on the metal chopsticks and spoons my father had set on the table.

"Can you believe it?" my mother said. "Your brother's almost here."

"He's just visiting today, isn't he?" I asked.

My father explained that my brother's visit was special because he was considering moving to Seattle. My brother might look for a place and work near our family.

"Your brother's been talking about Seattle," she said. "Maybe he sees how we are, and he wants to be with us. Maybe he's getting sick of California."

When my brother came through the door, he hugged everyone. My mother wept, "My son, my precious son." We gathered around the table with bowls of rice cake soup.

"I'm so hungry," my brother said. He looked tired from his flight.

"Help me." My mother pointed at the backyard door.

I opened the sliding door to air out the kitchen.

We tasted our soups together. "What do you think?" my mother asked.

"Mm," my brother said. "It's the best thing you ever made."

"She never makes it for me," my father said playfully. "Only for her children—"

My mother laughed. "I do enough things for you." She took a bite of her rice cake. "I'm good at cooking, but sometimes, I surprise myself. This is delicious."

My father said that even he was surprised, and my mother slapped his arm.

She got up from the table. "I also made short ribs," she said, and used scissors to cut the fat off the ribs before piling them on a plate. She threw more ribs on the pan and started a batter for her kimchi pancakes. The pepper flakes swirled in a creamy mixture.

My brother asked me, "How do you like Seattle?"

"You know what I like about it?" my father said.

"I was asking Eun Ji," my brother teased him. "It's not always about you."

My mother cackled. "Now that your son is around, you're not the boss."

"When my wife is around, I'm never the boss." My father pretended to cry, but he stopped and checked the rice cooker. With eyes bigger than his stomach, he packed four large bowls of wholesome, chewy rice for the table.

"Did you find a place yet?" I asked my brother.

He said, "I need a temporary place until I can find a better one. I don't want to rent again, but it's better than settling for any place right now."

My mother paused, then shared a glance with my father.

My father cleared his throat. "So, you're coming for sure?"

"No," my brother said. "Nothing's been decided——"

"Maybe you'd want to live across the city like me," I said. "You can stay at my house. There's a room downstairs with a bathroom and shower. You can take the garage, too."

"Oh!" my father said, putting his spoon down. "That's a great idea."

"That's exactly what I was thinking," my mother said. "You guys can live together." She fried a batch of kimchi pancakes and tore off an edge to try for herself. She told us it was spicy and salty and delightful.

My brother accepted, but insisted, "I would pay rent of course."

"Of course," I said. "Every month——"

"Aren't you supposed to refuse at first?" my mother scolded me. "You're his sister. You can at least offer to let him stay for free."

"She is *your* daughter," my father snapped at her. "You are in no position to complain about her when our son is coming. We're all together again——"

I did not respond. It occurred to me to wonder if I had ever told anyone, "Let's stop all this—before we can't undo it," could it have changed anything? It might be true that one's suffering and the suffering one has caused are the same.

The phone rang for my mother and father.

My father rushed outside, then returned to announce that they had to get back to the motel. Something had happened. It needed their attention.

"Oh no," my mother said. She covered the bowls, the plate of ribs, the pancakes, and the batter with cling wrap. "Then we'll eat when we get back. We won't be too long." She hurried to the door with her coat while calling out to us, "Don't touch anything. Leave everything as it is. When I get back home, we'll eat together, and it'll taste so good."

"Oh my God," my brother said. But he laughed.

We followed our parents out to the driveway.

My mother stopped and asked me, "Are you still scared of cars, Eun Ji?"

"It's getting better," I said, "on its own."

"You know, *my* mommy. She would've loved you," my mother said. "Now that you're older, I have somebody to talk to. I've been waiting forever. I'll tell you everything about my life. When you have a daughter, you'll think of me and say that's how it must have felt then. But you don't have to forgive me because you are my daughter. You don't have to do anything for me, okay? I was born to do everything for you."

When my father started the car, I embraced my mother's hand. There was a feeling that came back to me, and it was strange to sense that she must go.

Then, I let her go.

It was the first time.

ACKNOWLEDGMENTS

My thanks to Kate McKean who was steadfast and certain. To Elliott Stevens who was an inexhaustible reader and research guide. For their precious time: Crystal Hana Kim, Joseph Han, Zahir Janmohamed, and Ian Sanquist. I am bowed by the attention and care taken by Masie Cochran, Craig Popelars, Elizabeth DeMeo, Anne Horowitz, Allison Dubinsky, Nanci McCloskey, Molly Templeton, Jakob Vala, Yashwina Canter, and everyone at Tin House Books.

I am grateful to Bruce Cumings and Sonia Ryang for their scholarship; to those authors and researchers who came before me. I am indebted to Don Mee Choi and Emily Jung-min Yoon for reading my translations. Dr. Nicholas P. Reder fact-checked on short notice. I owe Sandra Silberstein for her Discourse Analysis instruction. Richard Block inspired new ways of seeing autobiography. Min Jin Lee encouraged me to reveal myself. James McMichael's poem "The Vegetables" was the beginning.

My mother spoke often of Jun and Lee throughout our lives. Though a few place Kumiko in mainland South Korea during the campaign, I place her on Jeju Island during her father's death. The details of hiding on the mountain and the argument with Kumiko's mother that led her father to be stoned were recalled by those who heard them from Kumiko. Some cannot be sure whether her father was stoned by South Korean police or extreme anti-Communist or Communist groups. One thing that remains certain is that he was innocent.

READER'S GUIDE

1. "The present is the revenge of the past." How does Eun Ji's opening line carry on through the rest of the memoir?

2. One of the themes of *The Magical Language of Others* is the idea of mothering in absence. In what ways does the relationship between Eun Ji and her mother change after her mother moves back to Korea? In what ways does Eun Ji's mother continue to raise her daughter, and in what ways does Eun Ji raise herself?

3. Of her mother's letters, Eun Ji writes, "Her letters are a one-way correspondence. The thought of writing her was unbearable." Have you ever received a message and felt that you couldn't write back?

4. The letters often talk about the subject of beauty and appearance. How is the subject of beauty handled across different cultures? How do expectations regarding beauty differ between Korea and the US, and in what ways are they the same?

5. Over the course of this memoir, Eun Ji's identity is informed by her experiences in America, Korea, and Japan. In what ways do you think each place impacted Eun Ji? In your own life, which places have impacted you most?

6. What does it mean to be a woman across different cultures and generations? What are the restrictions and freedoms shown in the book?

7. In telling her story, Eun Ji looks back at her grandmother Jun's life in Daejeon, and her grandmother Kumiko's experiences during the Jeju Island Massacre. In what ways do you think these histories shaped Eun Ji, and in what ways do you think your own family's history has shaped who you are?

8. Compare the lineage of Eun Ji, her mother, Jun, Kumiko, and Kumiko's mother. What beliefs do these women share and where do they disagree? Who does Eun Ji most resemble or not resemble at all?

9. After reading her poems, Joy says to Eun Ji, "You don't have to forgive your mother. I'm not telling you to forgive her. But the poem must forgive her, or the poem must

E. J. KOH is the author of the poetry collection *A Lesser Love*, winner of the Pleiades Press Editors Prize, and co-translator of Yi Won's *The World's Lightest Motorcycle*, forthcoming from Zephyr Press. Her poems, translations, and stories have appeared in *Boston Review*, *Los Angeles Review of Books*, and *World Literature Today*, among others. She earned her MFA in Literary Translation and Creative Writing from Columbia University, and is completing the PhD program at the University of Washington in Seattle. She is a recipient of Mac-Dowell and Kundiman fellowships.

thisisejkoh.com

forgive you for not." Do you agree with Joy? What role does forgiveness play in poetry? What role do you think forgiveness plays in Eun Ji's memoir?

10. Why do you think the title *The Magical Language of Others* was chosen for this book?